VASILIS PAPAGEORGIOU

Sunseekers or Dimming the Sun or

MIRELA
Baciak

Are We Under the Same Sun?

As we began to develop the exhibition *Sunseekers or Dimming the Sun or*, Vasilis Papageorgiou and I started from distinct perspectives. My thinking at that time was influenced by the impact of climate catastrophe on human health, both mental and physical, while Papageorgiou was concentrating on the role of labor within a capitalist framework. Over time, our perspectives converged, culminating in an exhibition focused on intertwined cycles of leisure, labor, and exhaustion.

It is June 2, 2024, as I write this text—*nomen omen*—the moment of seeking the sun. And so, while being temporarily in a different context than that of Salzburg, where the show took place, I ask myself if we are all indeed under the same sun, or if it shines differently depending on where we economically stand in society.

In *Sunseekers or Dimming the Sun or*, the sun served as a universal yet contradictory symbol, akin to water in its ubiquity and essentiality. Although the sun cannot be confined within national borders, it can sometimes divide us. It highlights harsh global inequalities, illuminated by the disproportionate impact of climate change on the world's poorest, whose ecological footprint is so minimal that their disappearance would barely alter climate processes. The exhibition cleverly contextualized the sun, navigating its ambiguities and drawing attention to the varied contexts under which it shows us the world.

A key work was a looped video presented on three screens suspended from the ceiling showing an elderly woman in front of a house in Albania, a bucket of water in her hands, as tourists pass by. With a deliberate motion, she casts the water onto the ground, the liquid arching gracefully. This act may seem mundane, perhaps a method to quiet the dust or cool the dry ground, but it could be a ritual of farewell—a traditional gesture in the wake of departing guests, symbolizing a wish for their safe journey and a hope that they, like water, will find their way. Another looped video in the exhibition, embedded in a metal sunbed, transported viewers to the Place des Vosges in Paris, showing children playing in a fountain during a heat wave. Despite the clearly different geographical and economic contexts, the elderly lady in Albania and the children playing in the Parisian fountain seem to have something in common—namely the search for moments of cooling relief.

It might be that exhaustion and the need to escape have become markers of our shared human condition, transcending individual circumstances and binding us together in a collective narrative of fatigue and the relentless pursuit of respite. Yet, as mobility and travel have evolved from privileges of the elite to widespread social expectations, the initial thrill of such freedoms has given way to a deeper understanding of their costs. This transformation reveals a seamy side to our conquest of leisure: the very mechanisms that enable our escapes also entrench our fatigue.

Across the globe, from bustling cities to quiet suburbs, people are propelled to seek refuge from the daily grind. The driving forces of automation, urban anonymity, and the commodification of natural and cultural resources have created an environment where individuals are less participants in their own lives and more observers, moving through the days with mechanical predictability. The escape, once a luxury, has become a necessity—a critical coping mechanism to manage the mental and physical toll of modern existence.

This shared cycle of work, exhaustion, and escape highlights a paradoxical truth: while our destinations may differ, the underlying reason for our journeys—the need to restore what daily life depletes—is universally felt. The places we flock to, consuming their climates and landscapes as if they were therapy, are not just vacation spots but sanctuaries from the pervasive sense of depletion that marks contemporary life. People are increasingly questioning the efficacy of a system that offers freedom only in snippets and reintegration into daily life as a return to servitude. This growing dissatisfaction points to a deeper craving—a desire not just for time away from the everyday, but for a life that is integrally more fulfilling and free from the constant need for escape.

As we confront these realities, the recognition of our shared exhaustion could potentially inspire a more profound societal shift. It beckons us to reimagine how we structure our lives, work, and communities to foster an environment where the need for escape is not quite so acute, and where the balance between exertion and relaxation is not maintained by fleeing but by a more harmonious way of living.

This is where *Sunseekers or Dimming the Sun or* was also a modest attempt to redefine our understanding of tourism, encouraging an approach that is rooted in reflection. It pointed to the "or" spaces—interstitial zones where dichotomies dissolve and new possibilities emerge. Each and every work in the show challenged visitors to undertake deep personal introspection, promoting humility, knowledge, and empathy, and inviting viewers to embrace the open-endedness of our collective future. Ultimately, the works don't just ask if we are all under the same sun; they compel us to consider how we share that sun.

KOSTAS
Stasinopoulos

Sunset 2111

Kostas Stasinopoulos

The heat wakes me up.
Sheets drenched, you're gone.
The innocent part of the day, that first sun, has been
changing for a while now.
The noise of the island fills the room.
Dawn is no more.
The walls are covered in moisture.

The streets are busy with morning trade.
Salty air and petrol in my nostrils, the burning asphalt
opens my pores.
A lethargic morning interrupted.
You're not from here.
And somehow that's okay.
I pick up peaches, apricots, watermelons, and cherries.
I carry them with me.
Micro sculptures of joy.

Invisible lines of assembly have brought us to this shore.
Sea lilies, beach towels, plastic litanies,
and choke machines.
Human factories of excess longing and a respite that
fails to materialize in a blue expanse.
A breath, a break, a crack.
The virus wants us to give in.
Overworked, vocabulary runs through my head,
insufficient.
Another nonsense holiday.

Sunset 21 11

A stretch of white and bronze shapes unfolds
across this summer haze.
Everywhere I look I'm blinded, anything
I touch burns.
A monoculture of sunbeds assumes the form of my
boredom; salt forms rivers on your skin.
Bodies twisted, gestures muted, ice cubes
falling in a glass.
The repetition of the waves mimics internal
murmurs as they crash on fire.
The lithium in my pocket is heated.
Your memory is different from online.
I seem to remember you better this way.

Anything I say falls flat; you're not listening,
or I'm not making sense.
My palms are sweaty, my thoughts are scrambled,
I get shivers.
A wildfire ravages your skin as it sticks to mine.
Your promises glow like embers.
What did you say?
Dripping everywhere, I gasp for air.
I wonder how long we have until we collapse.
Like my body right now, like how I feel when
I think about you.
Fill it up, I want more.
Let it all burn; this delirium, this fever dream, is just
too good to say stop.

Kostas Stasinopoulos

We still have time for more.

Underwater my mind quiets.
I always miss the sea, even when it's cold.
Seasons require a sleight of hand these days anyway.
I dive in clear waters holding your hand.
We smile, it's warm, great, loving.
You're glowing.
Kids, laughing, jump from the marina in the distance.
Splash.
Rays deflect, enter the dark, scrambled, where we
might still be able to hide.
The Earth's saltwater denounces the harm you
have done.

Do you feel every awakening is doomed to fade?
Hearts begin to beat slower, silence lands on the sand.
You and I stay behind.
How can I distill the beauty I have felt into a gesture
I can show you?
A woman throws water on the street as we pass by.
Flowers grow through the cracked pavement.
The memory of your smile at sunset, a tear through
which to enter a world on fire.
Mourning the loss of a carefree self, a call to prayer
sounds in my ears.
Someday we will return to the stars.

Sunset 21 11

This violence isn't slow anymore; it rustles in
the undergrowth everywhere.
An orange light keeps me up at night; it leaves ash
in my lungs.
I try to cough out your shortcomings, but I fail.
An oil spill joins the darkness of the sea.
All of the metal on Earth is aglow, melting into
autophagic matter,
forming an incandescent bed for the body and
its leftovers.
The combustion lights up your eyes and the night sky.

A planet is a body,
even if it's burning.

15

* Following Vasilis Papageorgiou's ceramic sunset series and its
titling principle, the title of this text corresponds
to the sunset time of the day I finished working on it.

PETROS Phokaides

The Global Sunbed

What makes such a seemingly mundane object as a sunbed acquire global significance—indeed, come to embody some of the most pressing dilemmas of our times? Can such a thing, when introduced into the reflective mechanism of an exhibition, expose the imaginaries but also the material transformations in which it has been embedded? Beyond a banal plastic object for mass tourism or a piece of designer outdoor furniture evoking privilege and wealth, can the sunbed be a powerful storytelling device capable of turning our attention from the tourism industry's global inequalities and coastal ruination to rethinking leisure as a practice of repair and planetary healing?

Despite its variations, the sunbed's genealogies are hard to miss. The image of the reclining body on a piece of furniture that is neither quite a chair nor a bed evokes a liminal individual and collective experience. We may think of cure chairs on balconies of sanatoria dedicated to treating tuberculosis, or deck chairs on liners crossing the Atlantic, or the 1929 chaise longue designed by Le Corbusier, Pierre Jeanneret, and Charlotte Perriand as a "machine for resting"[1]—these are but a few instances of how, in modernity, an individual's mental and physical restoration has involved the reclining position of an idle body, with or without direct exposure to the sun. It was only after the end of World War II that the sunbed

1   Carmen Espegel, *Women Architects in the Modern Movement* (New York: Routledge, 2017), 208–9.

arrived as a piece of beach furniture paradigmatic of a "conceptual shift from 'leisure' as a health-restoring practice, largely within the confines of nation-states, to 'tourism' as an industry and a practice of mass-consumption integrated with internationalized politics anticipating our interconnected, globalized present."[2]

Situated within this context, the sunbed effectively mirrors the emergence of what I (with my coauthors) have written about elsewhere as the "global sunbelt." This notion aims to highlight the links between post-war tourism, sunny and sandy beaches, and the complex ways such a formidable imaginary drove architectural and infrastructural transformations across East-West and North-South divides that "dismantled existing landscapes and livelihoods (from agricultural plots farmed by Blacks in the American South to fishing villages in Sri Lanka) and replaced them with roads, engineered beaches, hotels, resorts, and golf courses that came to define the very idea of the 'sunbelt' in popular imagination."[3] An integral part of these infrastructures mediating relations between bodies and the sun, the sunbed facilitated global dynamics of transnational travel, capital flows, and the international divisions of

19

2 Sibel Bozdoğan, Panayiota Pyla, and Petros Phokaides, *Coastal Architectures and Politics of Tourism: Leisurescapes in the Global Sunbelt* (London and New York: Routledge, 2022), xxi.
3 Bozdoğan, Pyla, and Phokaides, *Coastal Architectures and Politics of Tourism*, xxiv.

labor set forth by the tourism industry. Owing to its transportability and scale—whether placed along a beach or a pool, under an umbrella or directly under the blazing sun—sunbeds helped to expand the spatial and symbolic reach of global tourism by associating leisure with values and embodied experiences that seemed to appeal to many: rest, laziness, playfulness, freedom, and, for the fortunate few, comfort, luxury, privilege, and isolation. In other words, sunbeds capture the socio-spatial tensions and inequalities that have been exacerbated rather than ameliorated by tourism's global spread.

If the sunbed evokes the right (of the body) to rest, in our current predicament, this right exists at the expense of other bodies' exploitation, their labor (sometimes) obscured by paradisial and leisurely imagery. The privilege of lying on the sunbed can embody tourism's extreme forms of racialized violence. In the Greek islands, for example, the eco-chic, all-inclusive resorts reserved for international travelers overlap with, if not depend on, the erection of life-threatening borders against the migrants, war refugees, and asylum seekers whose flows have intensified since the mid-2010s.[4]

20

4   Costa-Gavras's film *Eden à l'Ouest* (Eden in the West, 2009) highlights tourism's dark sides. The film follows a migrant's journey through Greece to mainland Europe. In the opening scene, the protagonist is seen stranded in a secluded nudist resort called Eden Club: Paradise, passing himself off as a tourist or as staff, only to be traumatized when he encounters the drowned bodies of his fellow travelers at a nearby beach, which becomes a spectacle for the duly shocked tourists.

In the growing tourist economy of Africa, wealthy and middle-class white visitors from the Global North seek to combine relaxation on tropical coastal landscapes with the pleasures of sex with Black and brown African bodies.[5] The racial and economic inequalities of (sex) tourism in this case, which highlight the persistence of neocolonial imaginaries of Africa as a "wild," "exotic," "dark" continent, are captured vividly in Ulrich Seidl's 2012 film *Paradise: Love*, which follows a fifty-year-old, middle-class woman from Austria to Kenya's beaches. Among the key scenes is one presenting a sandy beach divided into two zones, one occupied by a white, mixed-gender crowd relaxing on sunbeds oriented toward the sea, the other populated by local Black men ("beach boys"), standing tirelessly. Only the white tourists are allowed to cross the divide, which is demarcated with a low-height white rope tied on wooden poles constantly surveilled by the local police. Less alarming than the divide and the policing is the juxtaposition of relaxing (white) bodies and standing (Black) bodies, exemplifying the social, racial, and economic inequalities between tourists and locals.

A social movement that emerged on the island of Paros in 2023 and quickly spread to other tourist destinations in Greece targeted sunbeds and sun chairs

5   Sitinga Kachipande, "Sun, Sand, Sex, and Safari: The Interplay of Sex Tourism and Global Inequalities in Africa's Tourism Industry," *Journal of Global South Studies* 40, no. 1 (Spring 2023): 1–37.

as profit-generating tools that spatially and economically restrict locals' access to the shore. Employing traditional forms of street protest and more sophisticated mapping tools to show evidence of the illegal spread of sunbeds along beaches, it was dubbed by the media the "beach towel movement."[6] Whereas the sunbed has become the metonym of an unregulated tourist industry—the commodification of what were once common resources, rendering the beach an "operational socio-technical landscape"[7]—the beach towel is now a symbol of the locals' right to the shore and of leisure as a rudimentary and unmediated bodily experience in one's own home landscape. Even in the mainstream Greek media, this movement was portrayed in a positive light, inasmuch as the regulation of local abuses and illegalities would not challenge tourism as a national industry continuously proliferating airports, exclusive resorts, luxury villas, and infinity pools along the country's sunny and sandy beaches.

Seen as part of the global infrastructural network that is endlessly expanding to harness the sun, sea, and sand, the sunbed is unavoidably connected to

6   Niki Kitsantonis, "'No Space for Us': Greeks Fight Beach Takeover by Pricey Sun Chairs," *New York Times*, August 15, 2023, https://www.nytimes.com/2023/08/15/world/greece-beach-towel-protests.html.
7   George Papam, David Bergé, and Phevos Kallitsis, eds., *The Beach Machine: Making and Operating the Mediterranean Coastline* (Athens: Kyklàda Press, 2022), back cover.

tourism's "multiplying effects" of resource abuse and environmental problems, which are, ultimately, undermining local and planetary futures.[8] Yet the sunbed is not telling a story only of mass tourism, inequalities, and violence on human and other-than-human environments. Mediating a relation between the body and the sun, it is also an infrastructure that embodies an undergoing geo-historical shift, anticipating the coming of a "solar future." While being a product of tourism's extractive logic and the uneven distribution of Earth's resources and fossil fuels, the sunbed also embodies the promise of focusing upward, toward the sun, to find both a renewable source of energy and a renewal of any hope to repair our bodies and the planet.

23

8   Chang Jiat Hwee, Petros Phokaides, and Panayiota Pyla, "Multiplying Effects: Capital, Water, and Architectures of Tourism," *e-flux Architecture*, November 2023, https://www.e-flux.com/architecture/accumulation/533755/multiplying-effects-capital-water-and-architectures-of-tourism/.

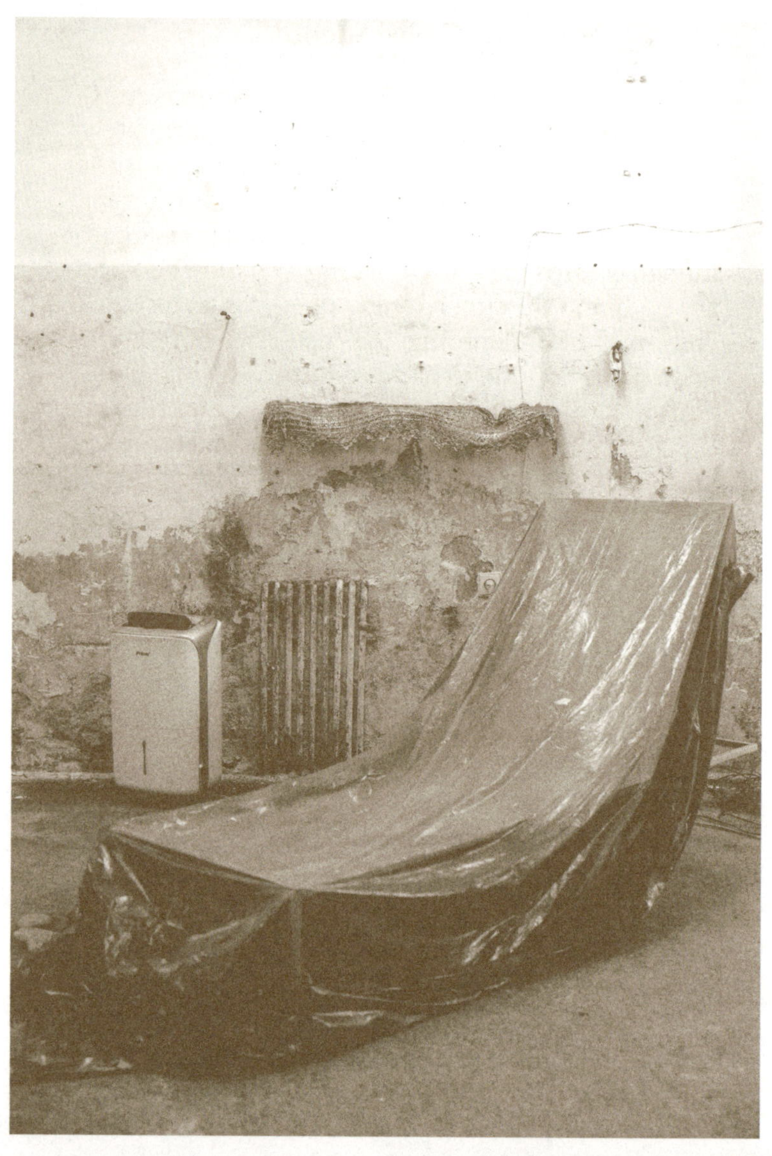

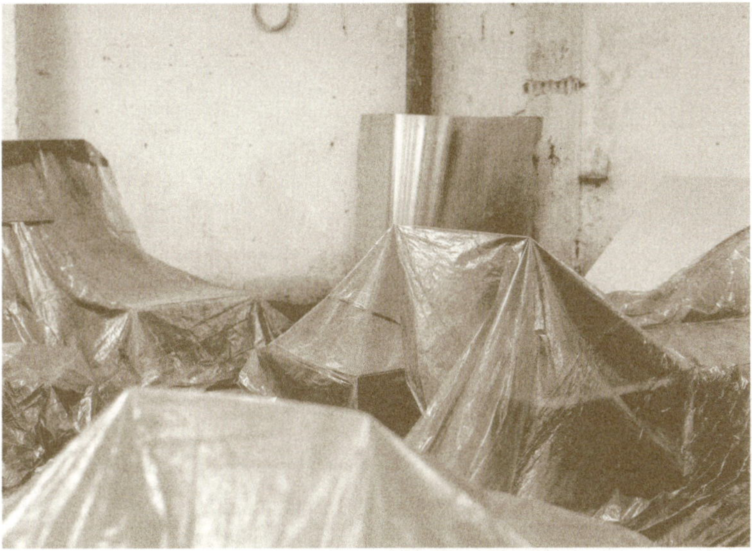

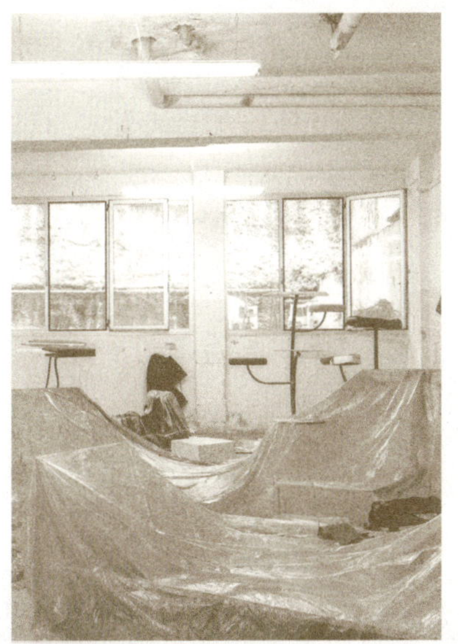

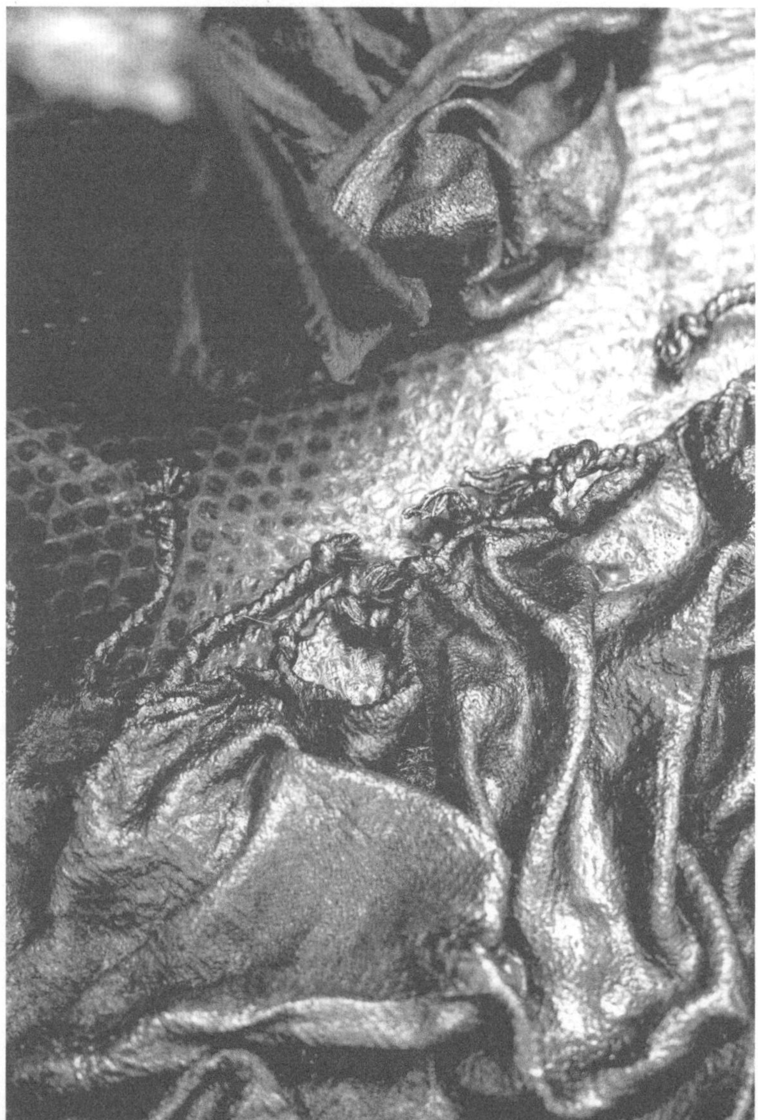

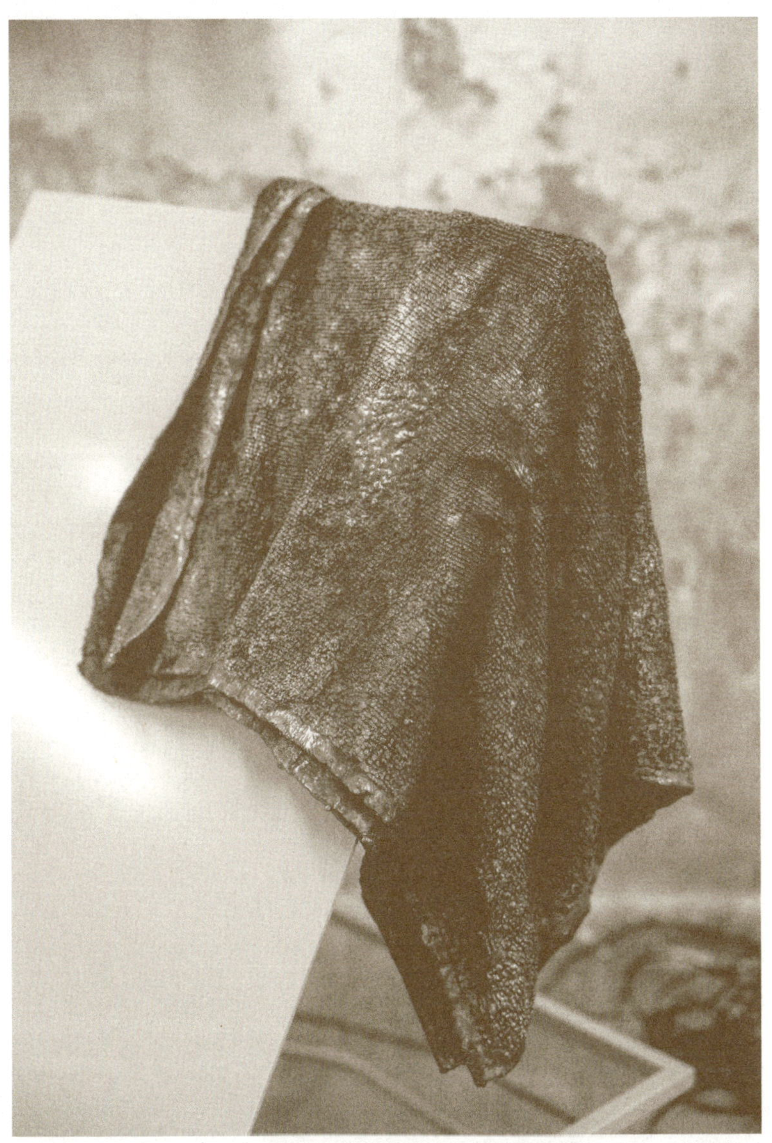

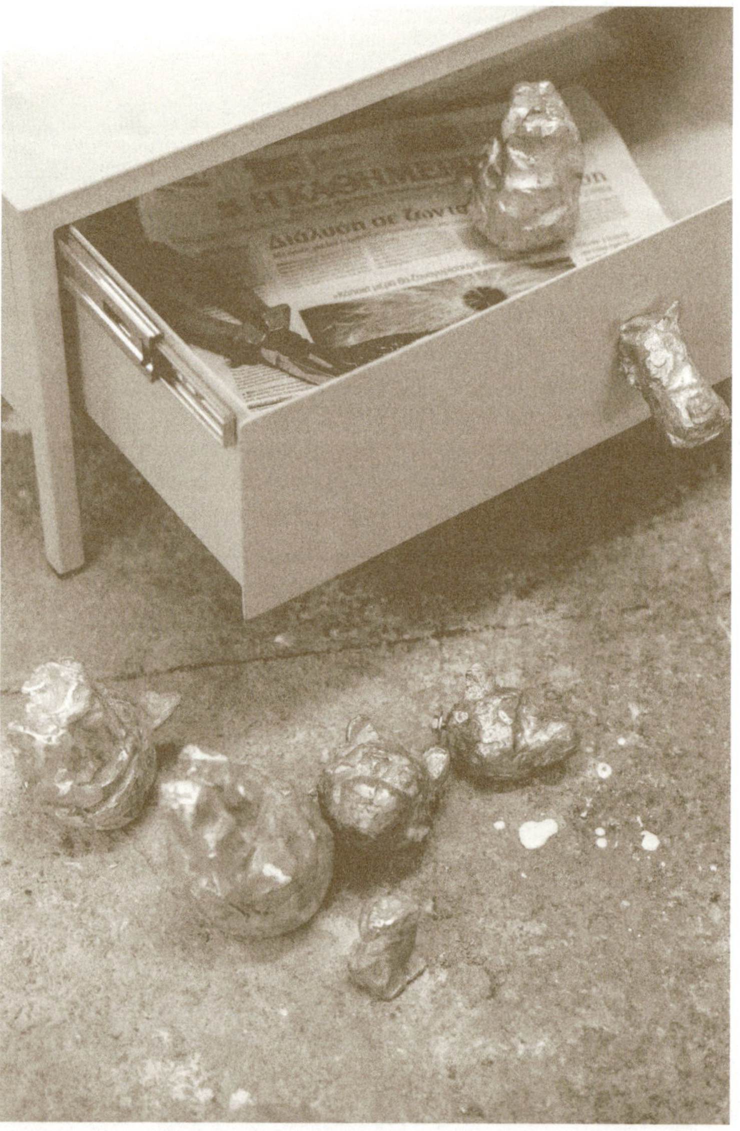

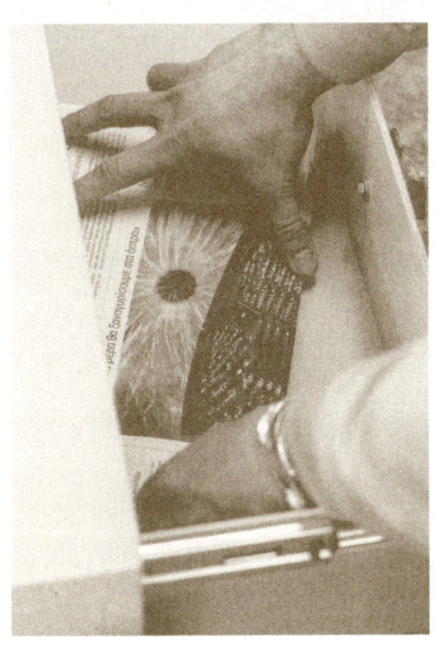
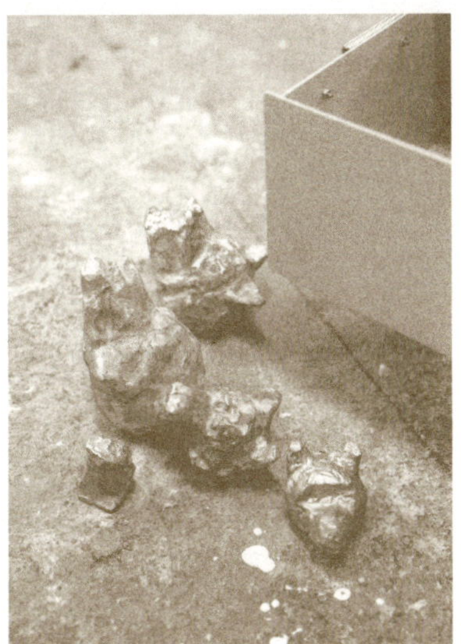

JULIA Morandeira Arrizabalaga

Tourism Apocalypse Now

Julia Morandeira Arrizabalaga

Most of us were suffering from various degrees
of beach fatigue, that chronic malaise which
exiles the victim to a limbo of endless sunbathing,
dark glasses and afternoon terraces.

—J. G. Ballard, *Vermilion Sands*, 1971

I doubt anyone will be surprised at what I am about to say, as, highly possibly, dear reader, you have experienced it in the flesh. We are in 2024, and the geographies of mass tourism are rapidly changing in Europe, the place from whence I write. Ravaged by scorching temperatures, uncontrolled extreme climate phenomena, and ubiquitous massification, the traditional "sun and sea" destinations are witnessing a drastic shift in the flux of visitors, who are trading their usual vacation spots for mountains and/or northern areas previously ignored. The sun-belt regions are ravaged not only by the impending and already-here effects of the climate crisis, but by decades of an extractivist economic model seeking to implant and sustain a predatory monoculture of hospitality and leisure.

While previously reserved for elites, tourism was developed for the masses in the West at the peak of modernity, hand in hand with promises of infrastructural development and economic growth in targeted regions and cities. Many countries around the global sunbelt were eager to adopt this industry, which provided tangible benefits during its first decades, but then calcified into a pervasive, inescapable, quite different reality. Yet today, amid financial and environmental crises and widespread recognition that the model is flawed, tourism continues to expand, justified by discourses of poverty alleviation, heritage conservation, or community impact through ethical spending, conscious travel, and other forms of "voluntourism."[1]

If the promise of tourism-led development has failed, how and why is it still held up as aspirational? Tourism monocultures, like other extractive industries, have been historically sustained by the provision of cheap labor—be it local or foreign, more or less visibilized, sometimes replaying old colonial genealogies of exploitation, but more often merely responding to contemporary forms of capitalism. In this all-encompassing economic landscape boosting full and immediate employment, local populations are cornered into an endemic proletarianization, entering the hospitality and leisure workforce at a young age and remaining stuck there, given the few alternatives to redress their trajectory as the government's disregard also becomes endemic, welcoming

1   A primary example of this is UNWTO's (United Nations World Tourism Organization) explanation of the vital role of tourism in its 2030 Agenda: https://www.unwto.org/why-tourism.

floating expat communities, for instance the so-called digital nomads, instead of training and investing in the local population so they might land those same tech jobs.[2]

However, and conversely, the tourism industry also becomes, in many cases, the only option to stay and resist an otherwise forceful economic displacement. As social anthropologist Matilde Córdoba Azcárate poignantly explains, tourism orderings of land and life are *sticky* for those who live off tourism or simply live in touristed places, because they are forms of entrapment: "They trap, capture, and entangle everyday rhythms, and with them, people's livelihoods and imaginaries. Tourism holds people in place and places in time. People get stuck in and with tourism's predatory orderings because tourism enables, even if only in the short term, the amelioration of otherwise precarious conditions of living."[3]

Both hosts and tourists become hooked on tourism in different but codependent ways, but their relationship has always been ambiguous, strained with conflict and

2 Blatant examples of this were the local government campaigns to attract foreign residents during the COVID-19 pandemic in places like Tenerife and Puerto Rico. As heard in Yaiza Hernández Velázquez, "Son[i]a #398: On Terminal Tourism," *Radio Web MACBA*, 2024, https://rwm.macba.cat/en/podcasts/sonia-398/.

3 Matilde Córdoba Azcárate, *Stuck with Tourism: Space, Power and Labor in Contemporary Yucatán* (Oakland: University of California Press, 2020), 16.

misrepresentation. The primacy of the "tourist gaze" still reigns, othering and consuming the local territory and its inhabitants.[4] The host's voice is also clearly heard. At the time of this writing, June 2024, protests against over-tourism are sweeping Spain, from the Canary Islands to the Balearic Islands and even Cantabria, a place previously undisturbed by tourist masses. The protesters are aligning their efforts with citizens' groups from cities such as Venice, Lisbon, Palma de Mallorca, and Barcelona, where locals have been drastically outnumbered by tourists. They ask for better regulations and moratoriums—not tourism's end, but its mitigation so as to regain affordable housing, public space, and quality of life. Simply put, as one of the placards reads: "To be able to survive where I was born."

35

4   John Urry coined the term "tourist gaze" in the 1990s to describe the structural connection between tourism and visual consumption: "The tourist gaze suggests that tourist experience involves a particular way of seeing. . . . Such visual and narrative depictions of tourist destinations are strategically promoted by the marketing industry to contrast with people's daily routine and work schedules at home. These imaginaries are captured through signs which signify a particular fantasy." John Urry, *The Tourist Gaze 3.0* (Los Angeles: SAGE Publications, 2011), 184. For Córdoba Azcárate, "This tourist gaze, as John Urry calls it, has become one of the most powerful orderings, defining and reifying patterns of inclusion and exclusion, gender and racial ideologies, and understandings about nature, culture, and society at large. In many parts of the world, tourism oversimplifies Indigenous bodies, politics, and places by promoting a kind of primitivism and pastoral exoticism used to reveal or conceal larger national market goals." Córdoba Azcárate, *Stuck with Tourism*, 16.

Nevertheless, the host-tourist relationship isn't always antagonistic. Thinking from her native Tenerife, transdisciplinary researcher Yaiza Hernández Velázquez signals how it is actually collapsing in many of these cheap holiday destinations, where the precarious classes from the North are being catered to by equally precarious classes in the South. Then, maybe, the issue at play is rather how to recognize our shared quality as hosts.[5]

Tourism is ripe with unfulfillable promises and paradoxes difficult to escape. It operates as a monocultural economic vortex attracting (cheap) labor, services, imaginaries, and narratives. In a predatory manner, it relinquishes the land and its population's present and futures to financial caprices, corporate agendas, and chronic dispossession. And even so, hosts are stuck in a vicious industry that brutally drains them, and guests are addicted to their two weeks in the sun, hoping it will dissipate their incurable dissatisfaction with life back home. It is a constellation of toxic attachments, messianic narratives, and compensation logistics, where affective economies of desire, hope, and despair run rampant, greatly informed by the imaginaries of escape, "freedom," social and cultural distinction, class aspiration, and mobility that tourism represents. For Hernández Velázquez, the apt adjective that defines tourism is "terminal": an endtimes,

5   Hernández Velázquez, "Son[i]a #398: On Terminal Tourism."

apocalyptic reality that, despite coming to terms with its untenability, we are incapable of letting go.

This uncanny combination of lure and disarray is sharply conveyed by the *Sunseekers or Dimming the Sun or* exhibition: its ample, deserted space, dotted by the yellow sunbeds imposing their homogeneously shiny color-block surfaces, akin to a ravaged, sun-drenched horizon devoid of human figures. Here and there are also symbols of promise and attachment, like the bronze ring recalling a cheap plastic souvenir or the flower sprouting from a sunbed. But the sticky, viscous ambivalence of tourism is most beautifully encapsulated in the video looming over the exhibition, in which a woman in Albania—a fast-developing tourist hot spot—sprinkles water as tourists pass by to say goodbye and wish for their safe return. As the camera focuses on the face of the woman in contrast with the indistinct mass of passersby, conflicted emotions well up, but the essential one is likely discomfort. The underlying question is whether we observers identify as hosts or guests—or both.

Like tourism, contemporary art as it developed during the last half of the twentieth century promised experiences of discovery, encounter, and exchange among different cultures and contexts. Both became organized into geographies of privilege, legibility, and visibility that regularly intersect. Meaning making is the business at hand: narratives of self and other, conceptions of past and future, dreams of natural and cultural encounters, all generated through desire, anticipation, and memorabilia.[6] But tourism, at the moment, doesn't offer the same means as contemporary art to generate emancipatory or visionary speculations. Geographer and writer George Papam articulates the pervasiveness of the monocultural imaginations of tourism as a Fisherian tourist realism—"difficult to escape and difficult to unthink"—co-opting even the imaginaries that attempt to surpass it. His proposal: "For all their persistence, infrastructures of tourism and hospitality are perhaps easier redirected and 'put in reverse' than countered. Then, the cultural and political work necessary is not only this of negation and resistance, but also that of bold reconceptualizations and reimaginings. Programs that pluralize the current monocultures of tourism are necessary, but perhaps even more essential are ideas that are disruptive. . . . An anti-anti-utopian habit of mind, that is bold as it is absurd."[7]

The question is, then, an eternal one: As cultural workers, what is to be done? Maybe short-circuit the production of tourist affects and compensatory

6   Córdoba Azcárate, *Stuck with Tourism*, 6.
7   Gregor Papam, "Hospitality Fatigue: Symptoms and Potions," in *Islands after Tourism: Escaping the Monocultures of Leisure*, eds. Gregor Papam and David Bergé (Athens: kyklàda.press, 2023), 12.

imaginaries of leisure, to reimagine attachments and redirect desire beyond just-for-pleasure mobilities. Radicalize the practices and concepts of leisure and travel in non-indulgent and non-predatory ways. Or open up an arena where recognition between hosts and guests is enacted, and new imaginaries of solidarity deployed. Imagine an eco-social tax against the rapid cancellation of futures and the present debts enforced by tourism. Occupy the toxic hospitality infrastructure, and redirect it toward hospitable forms of climate mitigation. Escape the numbness of chronic beach fatigue toward emancipatory, more livable horizons. Endorse ultimately a full tourism apocalypse, following the Greek etymology of the word, which refers to its capacity for destruction as well as revelation. Invoke apocalyptic hospitality and leisure to reveal and destroy tourism as we know it and leave room for more pleasurable and hospitable worlds.

DANAI Giannoglou and VASILIS Papageorgiou

Sun Yellow or Coral Red or

DANAI GIANNOGLOU:
Let's begin with the ultimate conversation starter:
How's the weather where you are?
VASILIS PAPAGEORGIOU:
It's late May, and here in Athens it
is already warmer than what we're
used to at this time of year—28 degrees Celsius. However, my studio is
in an old semi-basement, which keeps
a cool atmosphere despite the heat
and humidity. In the past month, the
sky has often been orange because of
the Saharan dust clouds, but now it's
blue—clear blue and sunny.

DG:	When you need to squint your eyes because
of the glare, what do you think of?
VP:	At the preparatory class for Athens
School of Fine Arts, when we were being taught how to take the measure of
our painting subjects—to understand
their volume and proportions—they
told us to close one eye and hold out
our thumb as a measuring instrument.
So when the sun's glare is blinding me,
my brain remembers this and auto-
matically I try to simplify the forms
around me and the way they receive
or reflect the light. Your perception

of space changes vastly when your surroundings are momentarily reduced to their color characteristics.

DG: That's a rather painterly thought for a sculptor.

VP: I guess so, but it's also a sculptural simplification of forms—a way to understand the light, its sources, where it's dark and where it's bright and how the shadows are formed. The exercise I described is indeed a technique that can help you paint realistically, but basically it's a trick that allows for a better understanding of three-dimensional objects and shapes.

DG: Is "sun yellow" the color of good weather?

VP: It could be. It's a very interesting question. "Sun yellow" is the name of a specific color in the RAL palette: Sun Yellow 1037. This is supposed to be an international code to communicate colors, so most of them borrow their names from natural elements—"coral red," "sand yellow," "lemon yellow." The RAL system was created in 1927 by the German National Commission for Delivery Terms and Quality Assurance ("RAL" is the acronym for that in German). Initially it had forty colors, but it grew quickly. A question that arises for me is: How is it "safer" or more vernacular to speak about the natural equivalent of chemically produced colors, since nature has been changing rapidly, and obviously we don't all have the same intuitive references for it? I wouldn't call the color of sand "yellow," but then again I've only been to Mediterranean beaches. Corals have different colors in and out of the water. And what does "sun yellow" even mean? This particular RAL code seems closer to the color children use to depict the sun than that of the actual sun.

Then there is the issue of weather. I'm not sure what "good" weather even is. A tourist, a farmer, a delivery person, somebody who cannot afford the increasing prices of gas and electricity, and someone from Greece versus someone from Nebraska are surely bound to have different opinions. The weather has both purely aesthetic characteristics and tangible effects. I am interested in that space in between, thinking for example of the interwovenness of weather conditions and labor conditions.

DG: Speaking about weather relativity and labor, I am thinking of your exhibition's opening night. It was March 1, and we could see the snowy tops of the mountains surrounding Salzburg, a city three hours from Vienna and half an hour from the closest Austrian-German border. What does it mean to exhibit your sun-yellow sunbeds in a chilly central European City without a coastline?

VP: You're implying a contradiction, but I'm not sure there is one. That said, I have been trying to answer that very question, and this is why I often think of the route between coastal Greece and Salzburg through the lenses of nomadic populations but also tourists and "sun-seekers." The sound piece, composed by Dimitris Prokos, that was playing for a few minutes every hour during the exhibition is a sonic depiction of the musical traditions and immaterial legacies of this route, of this trip—a trip that crosses borders and flows between different and similar places and communities of the urban and rural fabric.

The sunbeds can also be metaphors for a precarious relationship to nature, and in many ways this relationship is not specific to only one place, or only the most obvious places. It is something that "travels" with us, with our identities, our decisions, our privilege, our class, and our struggles. Greece over the years has symbolized many things. But there is no south without north, and no sun belts without sunseekers, so an issue is not only relevant where the phenomenon in question occurs. Maybe even more interesting is to think of the circumstances that created it and what might follow. For example over-touristification, which is quite tightly bound to gentrification, is not only a "privilege" of the sunny coastlines; it's part of a chain of events, a cycle.

DG: Cycle and repetition are also essential to labor, which is a recurring theme in your practice, especially in its relationship with leisure.

VP: I am interested in the political aspects of what we call "routine," which for me is a continuous, systematized alternation between labor and leisure time. Sunrises and sunsets are on the one hand spectacular natural phenomena, but in many ways also the punctuations between these two times. *Sunseekers or dimming the sun or* (2024) touches upon this galloping industrialization of leisure time and the way it affects human and planetary resources as well as architecture. Leisure, especially if we see it through the prism of tourism development, requires infrastructure and labor, which simply means that for a person to relax and go on holiday, another person needs to work. This often creates a relational system where so many layers of social and environmental injustice become apparent.

My initial interest was in the architectural and spatial characteristics of the places where these dynamics appear, such as bars, but also in the public places where people rest, such as plazas and beaches. My sculptural interpretation of labor is becoming my own labor. In the series of works *Together we don't stand* (2021), I take as my starting point the form of a public bench, which becomes a host structure ready to receive the human body. In my sculptural vocabulary, such structures are at the same time welcoming and hostile.

Repetition is definitely part of my artistic practice as well. I usually work in series, which for me creates systems that function in complementary ways.

DG: From the scale of your work, but also your alterations of materials, it is obvious that you have technical collaborators. Collective labor comes up quite often when you discuss your practice—practically but also conceptually.

VP: Producing the work is what I enjoy the most. It's intense, sweeping, and so fulfilling. Materials, ideas, artworks—you know, they can resist you. Sometimes it's difficult to decode them. My collaborators are my teachers and my translators. They help me learn new languages, and at the same time they translate me and vice-versa. The translation from the initial idea to the potential form and back can serve wishes or meet needs, again through the prism of limitations—financial, material, scale-wise, et cetera. It's important to acknowledge that you cannot do everything, that there are experts who know much more than you do. I work consistently with the same people. Their touch, their voices, their ideas and solutions

are all over my work. They are insepa-
rable parts of my practice. For instance
the metalwork of Thanos Vasileiou is
everywhere in this project. And I would
never have been able to develop the
sunset ceramic technique if it wasn't for
the trust and tenacity of Daphne Leon.

DG: One element that we still haven't discussed is
the films in the exhibition. In the one that plays on
three separate screens, we witness a Balkan ritual en-
countered at a lakeside Albanian village. Do you have
a ritual of your own, either as a host or as a guest?
VP: Yes, I do. I hope to be both, constantly.
[laughs]

BIOGRAPHIES

DANAI GIANNOGLOU

is a curator, writer and editor living in Athens and Amsterdam. She is the co-founder and director of Enterprise Projects, an Athens based project space founded in 2015, as well as the editor of Enterprise Projects Journal, a publishing initiative by Enterprise Projects. Danai has held positions at de Appel, Amsterdam and at DESTE Foundation for Contemporary Art, Athens, and she has curated exhibitions, publications and programmes for various institutions and organizations. She was a participant of the de Appel Curatorial Programme 2019/2020 in Amsterdam.

KOSTAS STASINOPOULOS

is a curator and writer. He is Curator, Live Programmes at Serpentine, London, has served as Associate Curator at The Stavros Niarchos Foundation Cultural Center and has collaborated with the Whitechapel Gallery, White Cube, Frieze and the Athens Biennale. Kostas received his PhD in History of Art from University of York, funded by the Arts and Humanities Research Council, the Onassis Foundation and NEON. He holds an MA in History of Art from the Courtauld Institute of Art and a BSc in Biochemistry from Imperial

College London. Together with Hans Ulrich Obrist, Artistic Director, Serpentine, he is the co-editor of *140 Artists' Ideas for Planet Earth* (Penguin, 2021).

JULIA MORANDEIRA ARRIZABALAGA is a curator, researcher and educator. She is Director of KADIST Paris and teacher/organizer of the course Social and Ecological Justice Activism in the Visual Arts at Leiden University. Her practice is articulated in long-standing projects of curatorial research, which materialize in different formats and gestures.

PETROS PHOKAIDES received his architecture degree and PhD from NTUA, Greece. He is currently an assistant professor at the Department of Architecture, University of Thessaly where he teaches theories of architecture and design. His research focuses on architecture, infrastructures and broader landscape transformations to understand postcolonial visions, geopolitics, and socio-environmental change with a special focus on the Global South. He is the co-editor (with A. Chronaki) of the book *Theses of Memory* (Nissos, 2016) and (with S. Bozdoğan and P. Pyla) of the *Coastal Architectures and the Politics of Tourism: Leisurescapes in the Global Sunbelt* (Routledge, 2022). He is a founding member of Docomomo Cyprus and currently serves on the editorial team of the open-source, peer-reveiwed journal *Architectural Histories.*

VASILIS PAPAGEORGIOU

(b. 1991) is an artist working and living in Athens. Papageorgiou has showcased his work in various group and solo shows both in Greece and abroad. In 2024 he presented his first institutional solo exhibition at the Salzburger Kunstverein in Austria. In 2023, he was a resident at LUMA Arles and in 2022 he was awarded the Matteo Viglietta Award in Turin, Italy. His work is part of various collections such as the Onassis Foundation Collection and the Collezione La Gaia.

MIRELA BACIAK

(b. 1987) is a curator in the field of visual arts whose practice is guided by the notion of hospitality as a process which captures one's ethical relation to the unknown and the strange. Since July 2023 she is serving as the director of Salzburger Kunstverein. Before she was a curator at steirischer herbst festival in Graz from 2019–2023 and worked at Public Art Munich in 2018. Baciak holds an MA in Critical Studies from the Academy of Fine Arts in Vienna. In 2023, she initiated the AAC | Austrian Association of Curators, an organization that fosters curatorial-knowledge production.

ACKNOWLEDGMENTS

This publication marks the final act in a series of exchanges, track changes, research, patience and care. For all this I have to thank Mirela Baciak and Michaela Lederer, from Salzburger Kunstverein and Ilaria Bombelli and Gloria Favaro from Mousse, without whom this undertaking wouldn't have been possible.

I am humbled and grateful to Julia Morandeira Arrizabalaga, Kostas Stasinopoulos, Petros Phokaides and Mirela Baciak for their powerful research and their poetic reflections, and to their generosity of sharing them. I am also thankful to Danai Giannoglou for our conversation.

Paola Bonino, Marta Barbieri (UNA Galleria) and Olympia Tzortzi (Callirrhoë) as well as all the people who supported this book have been pivotal in its materialization and I would like to thank them sincerely for their trust.

Last but not least I want to thank my colleague, Mariana Antzoulatou who worked tirelessly and inspiringly both for the production of the exhibition and the publication.

Vasilis Papageorgiou

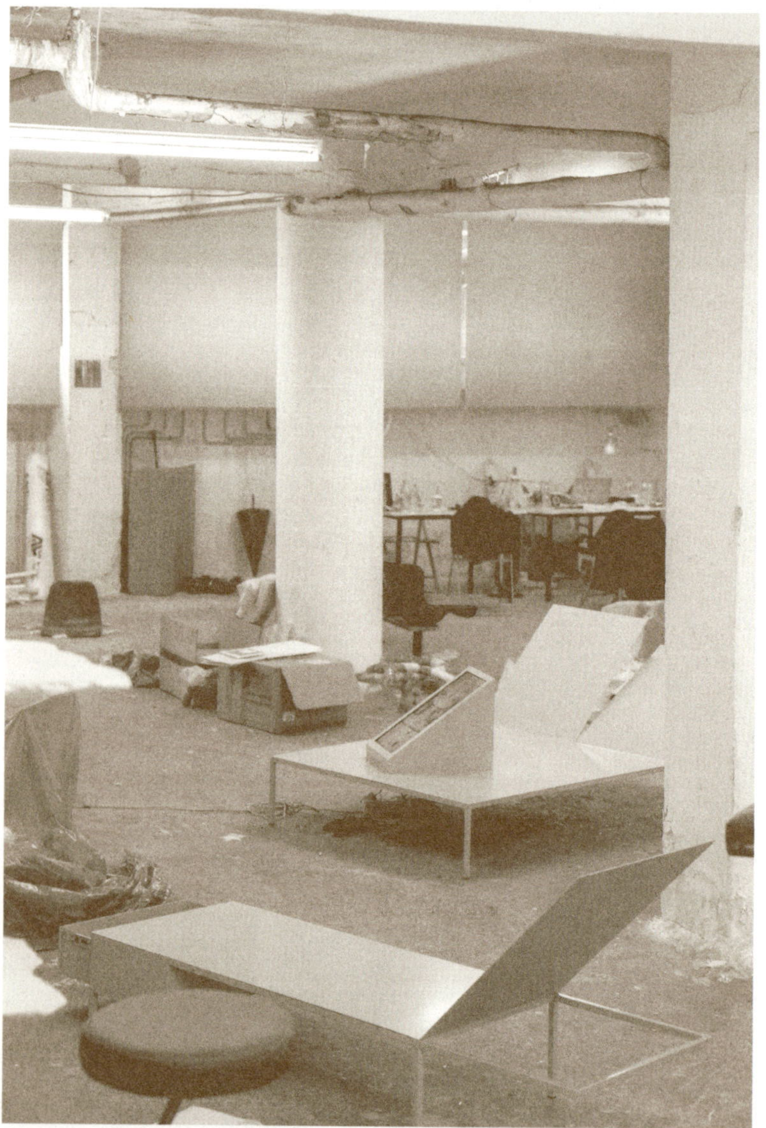

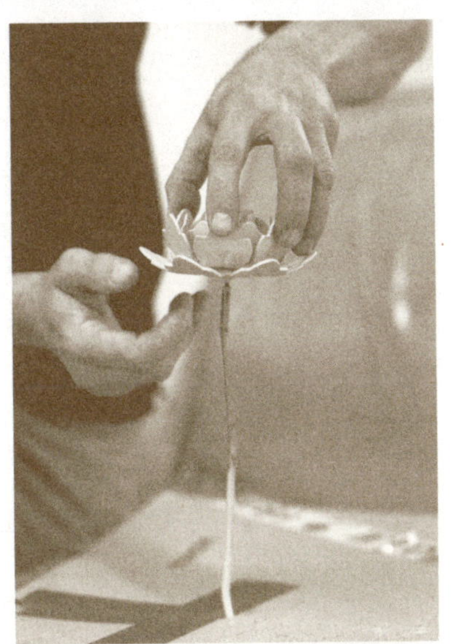

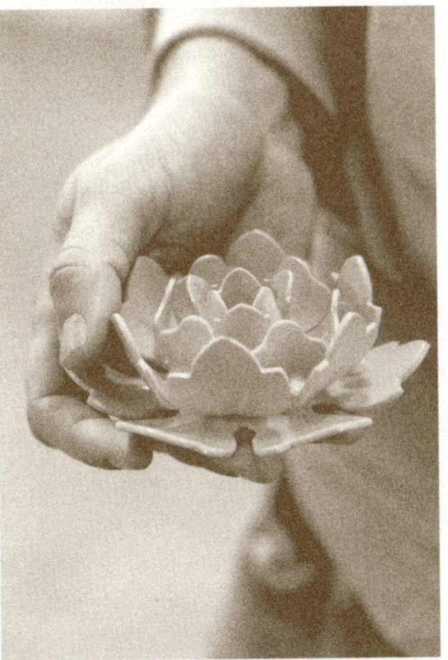

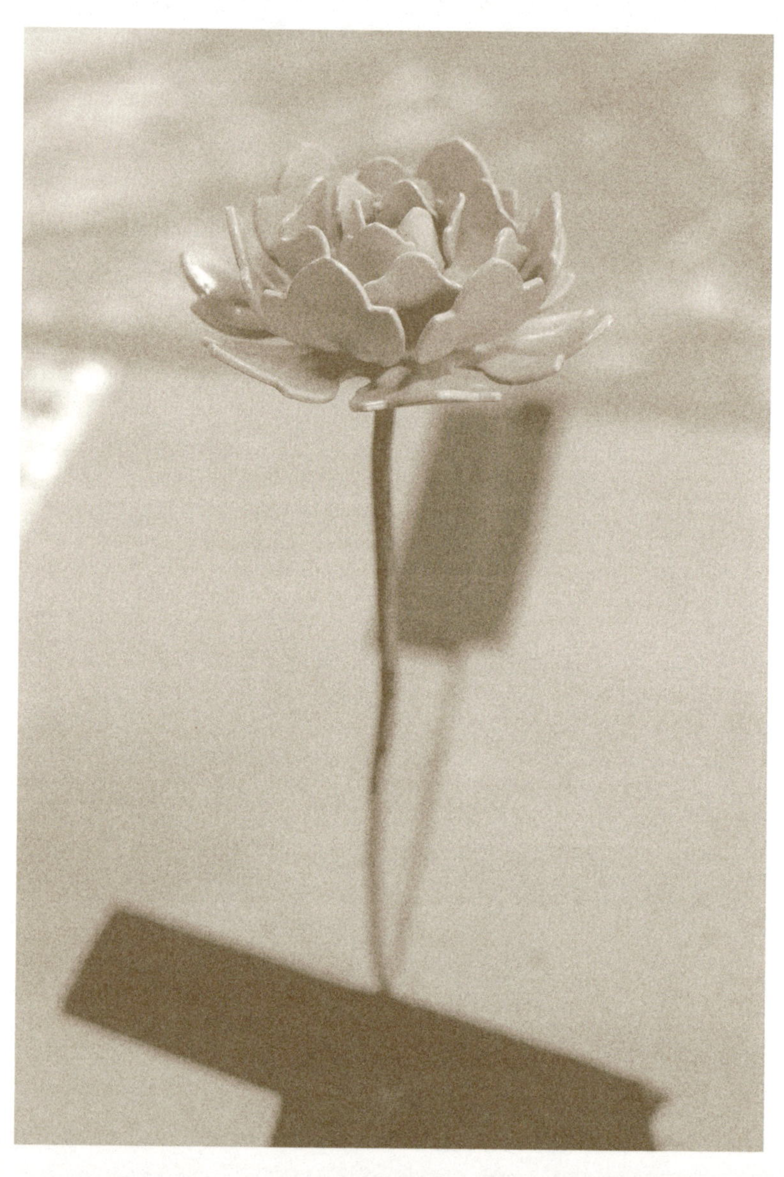

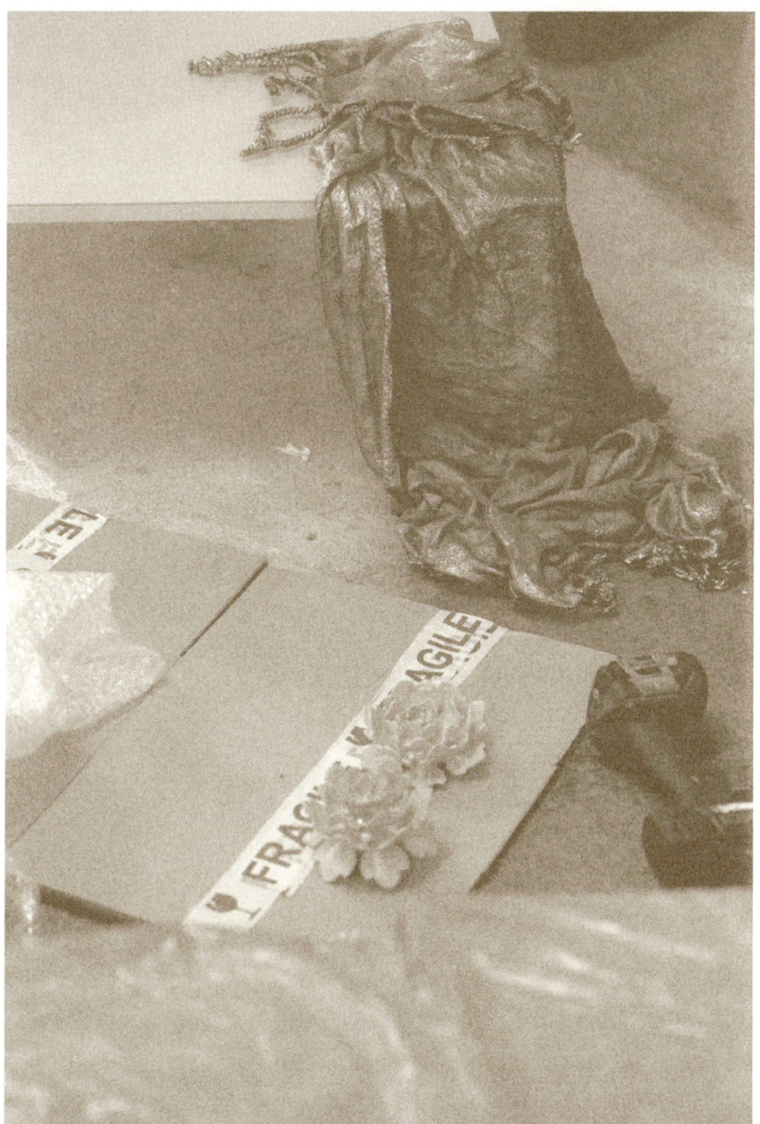
FRAGILE
AGILE
FRA

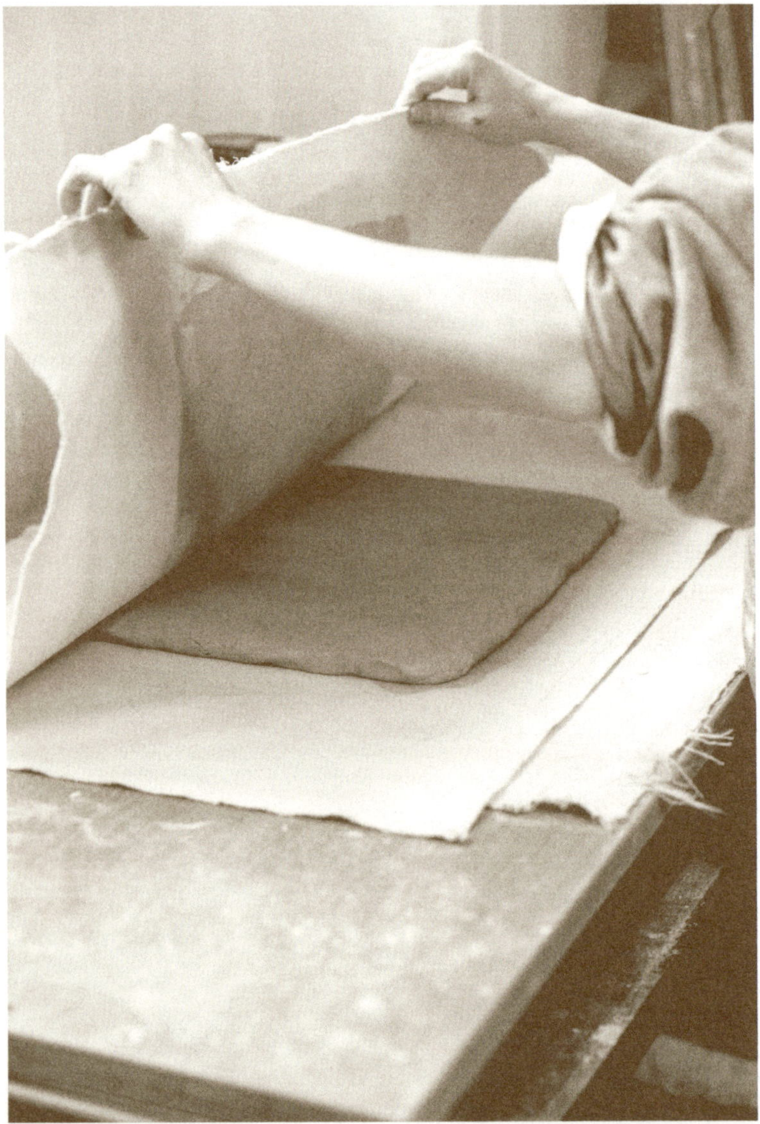

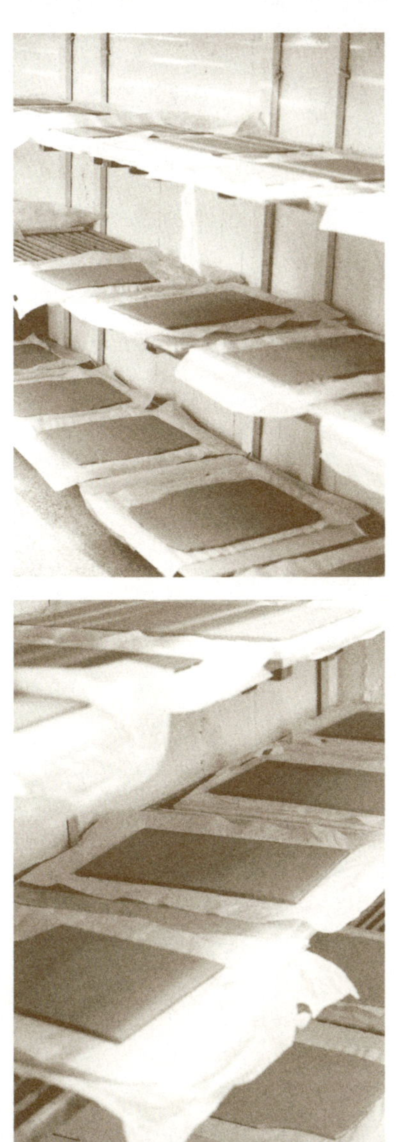

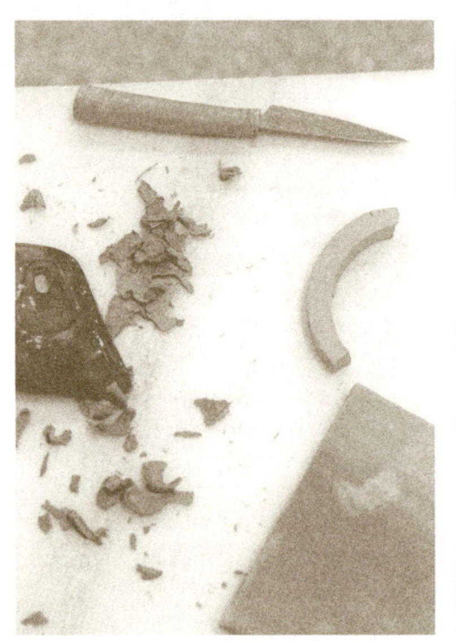 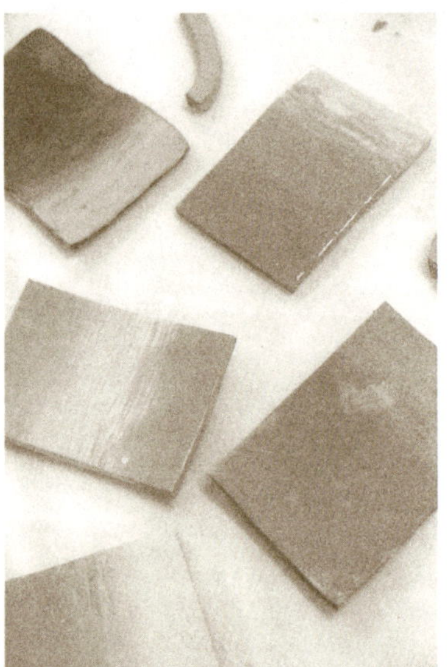

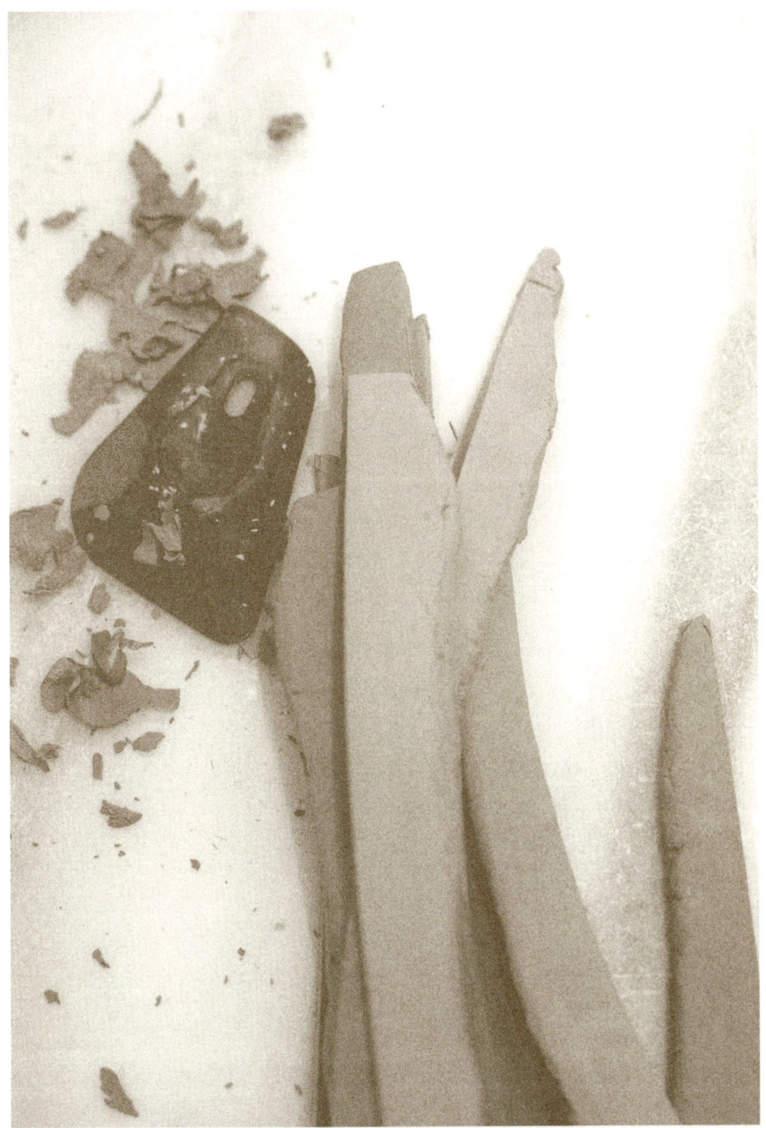

Sunseekers or Dimming the Sun or

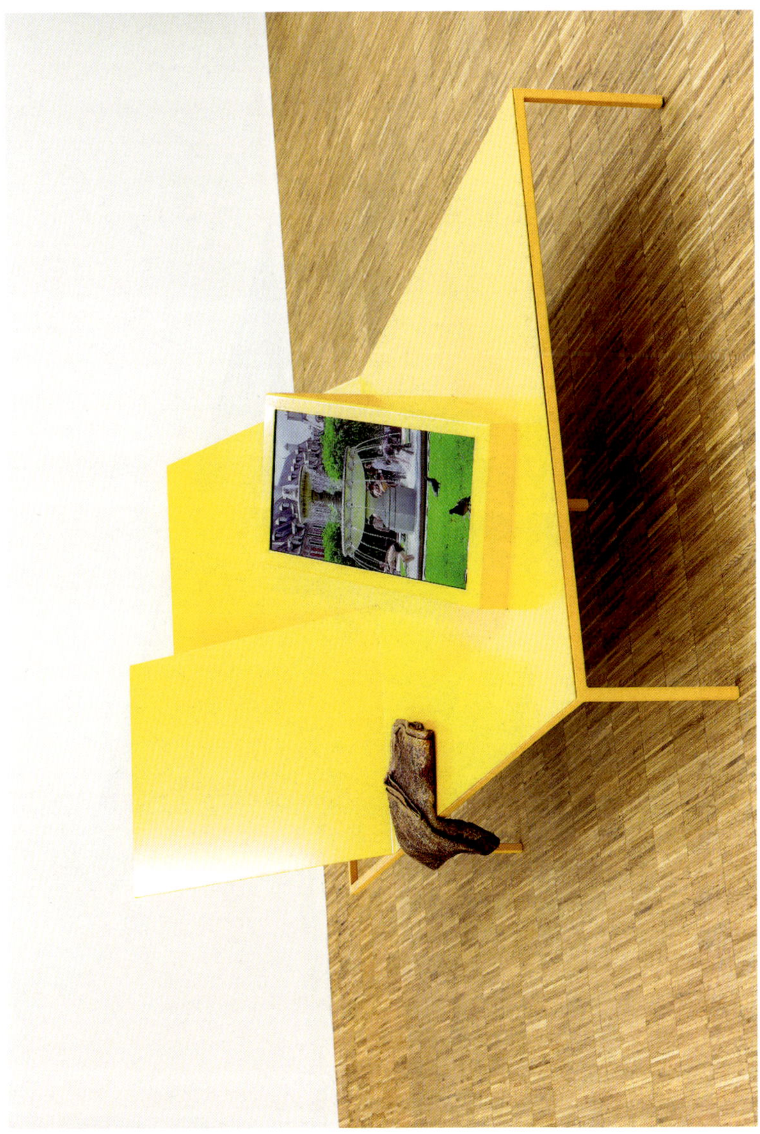

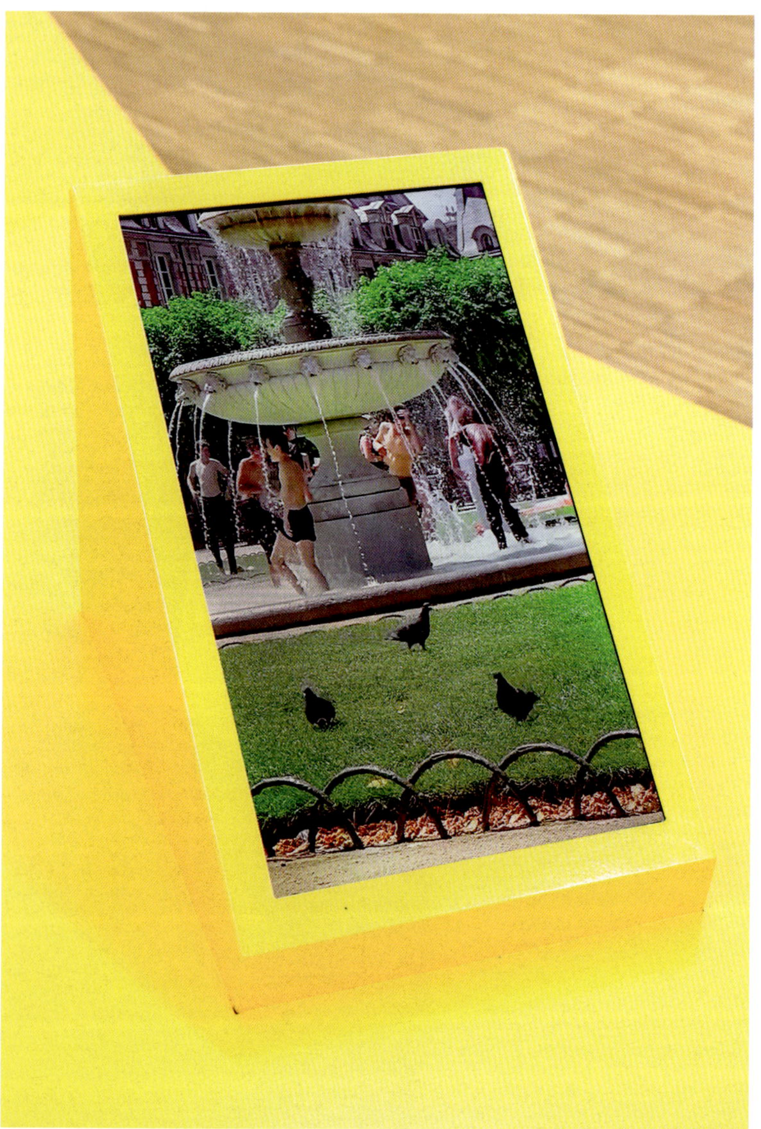

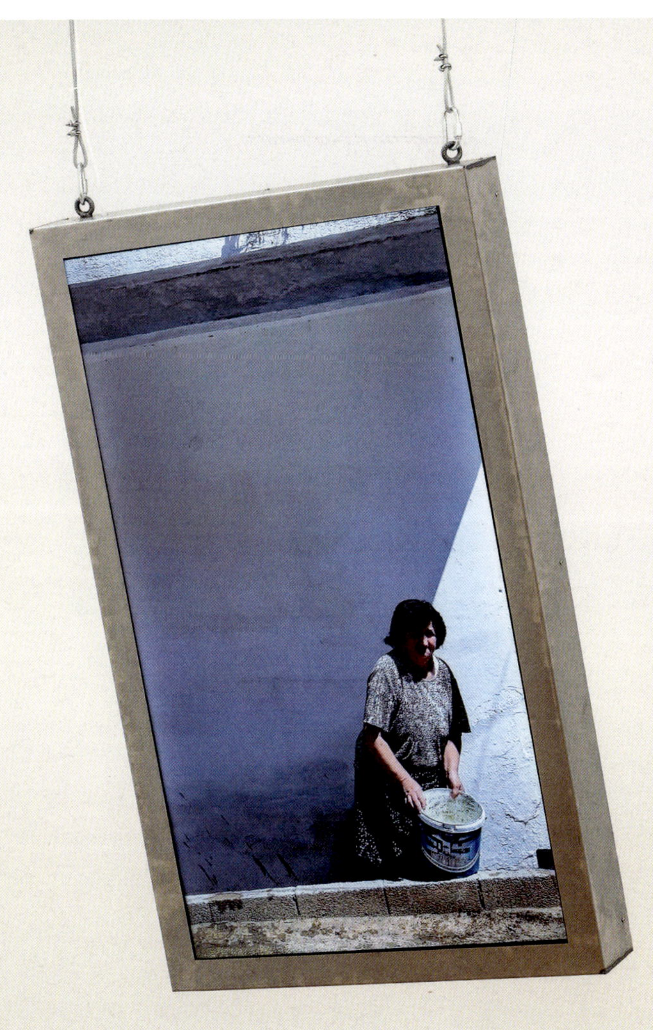

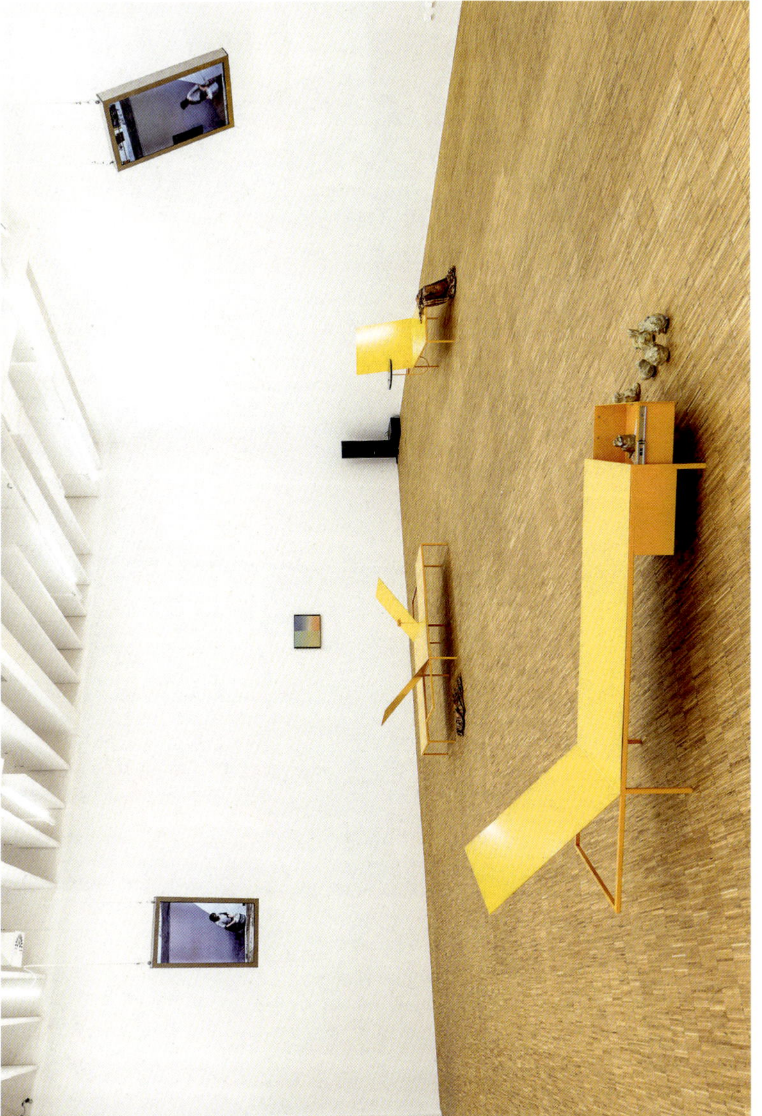

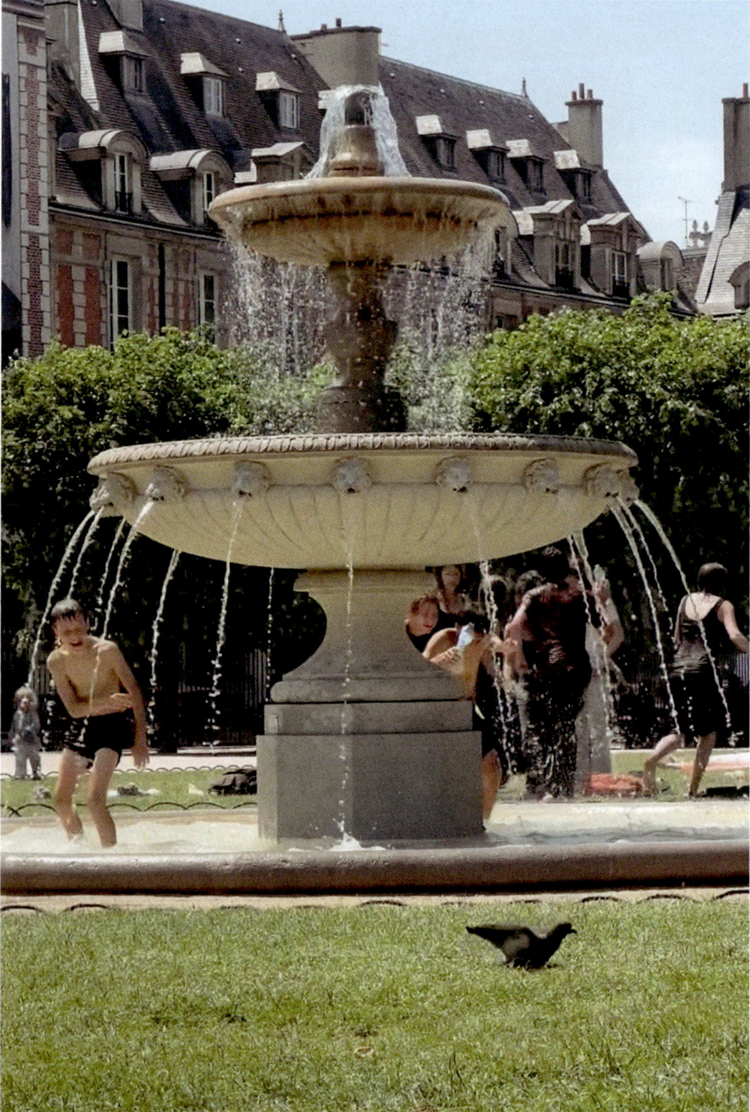

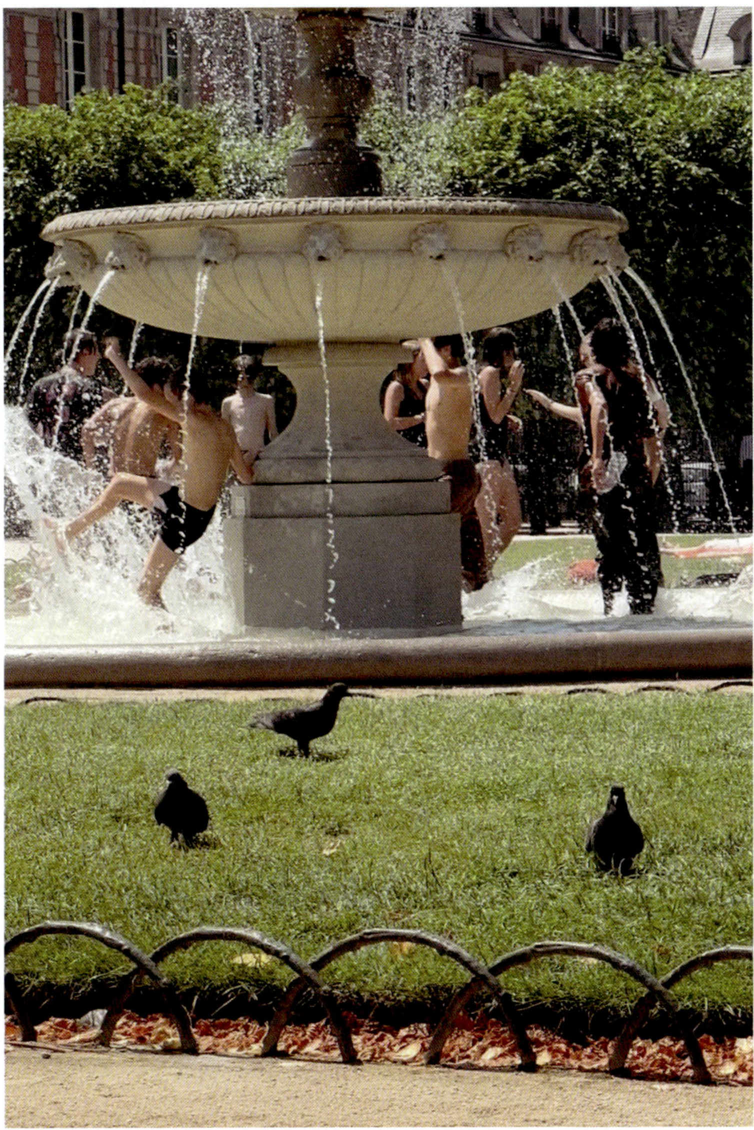

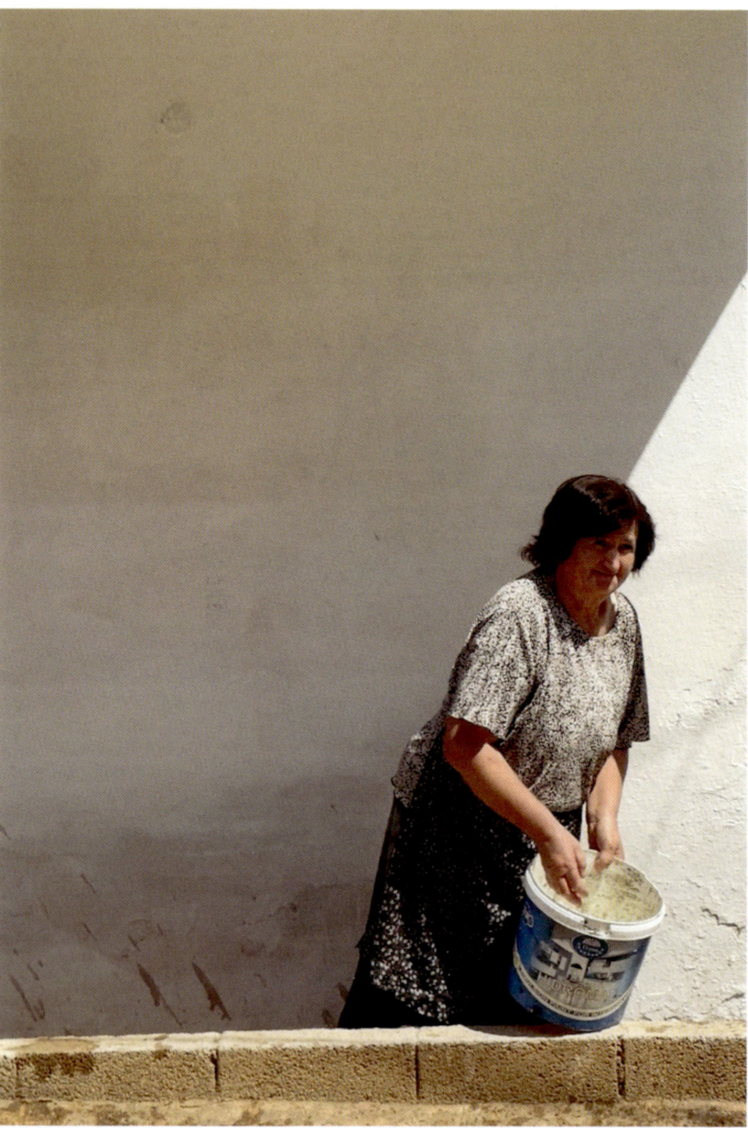

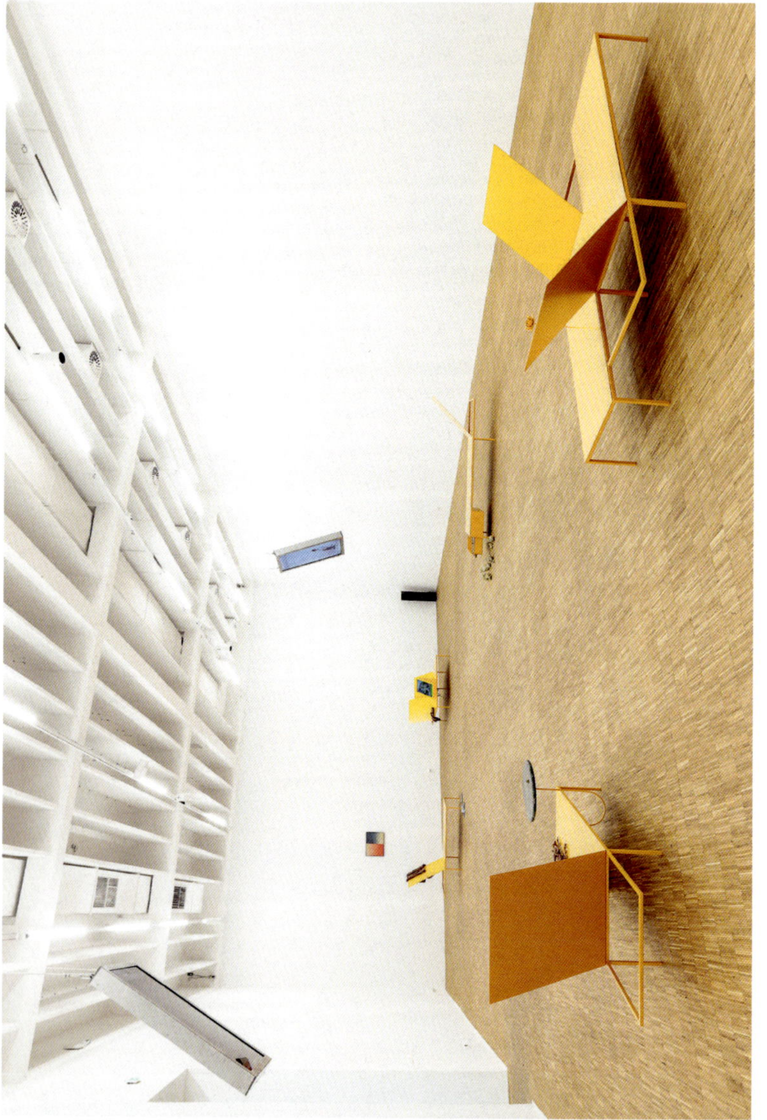

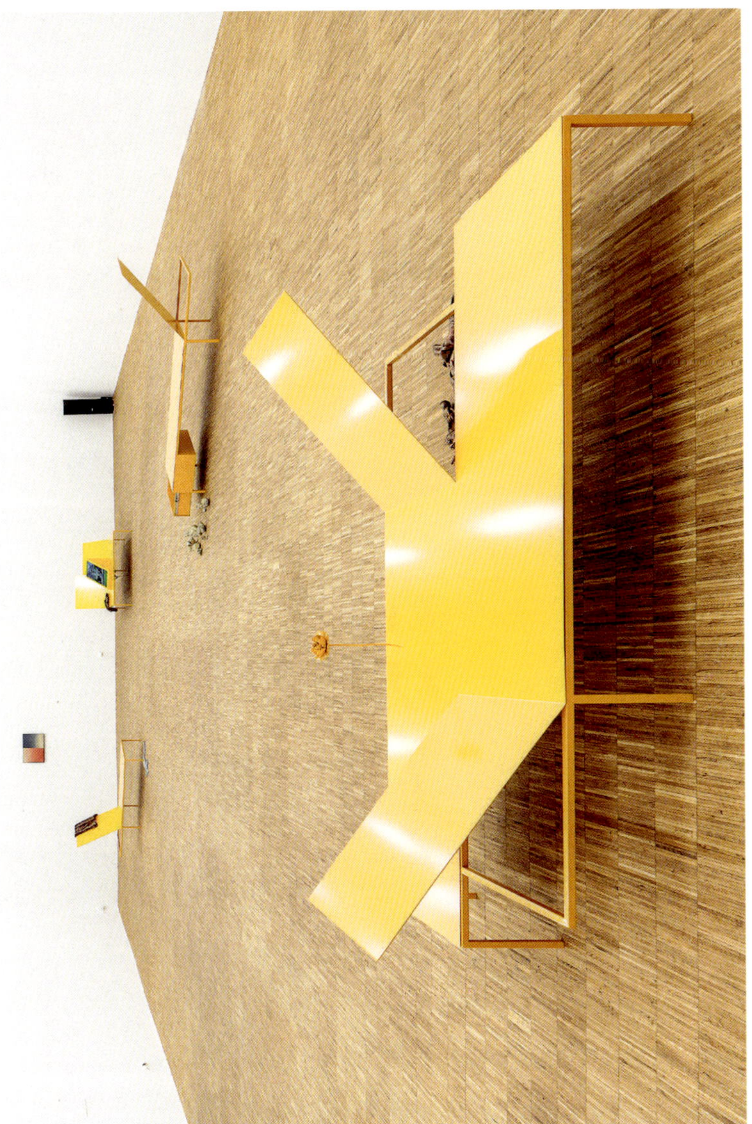

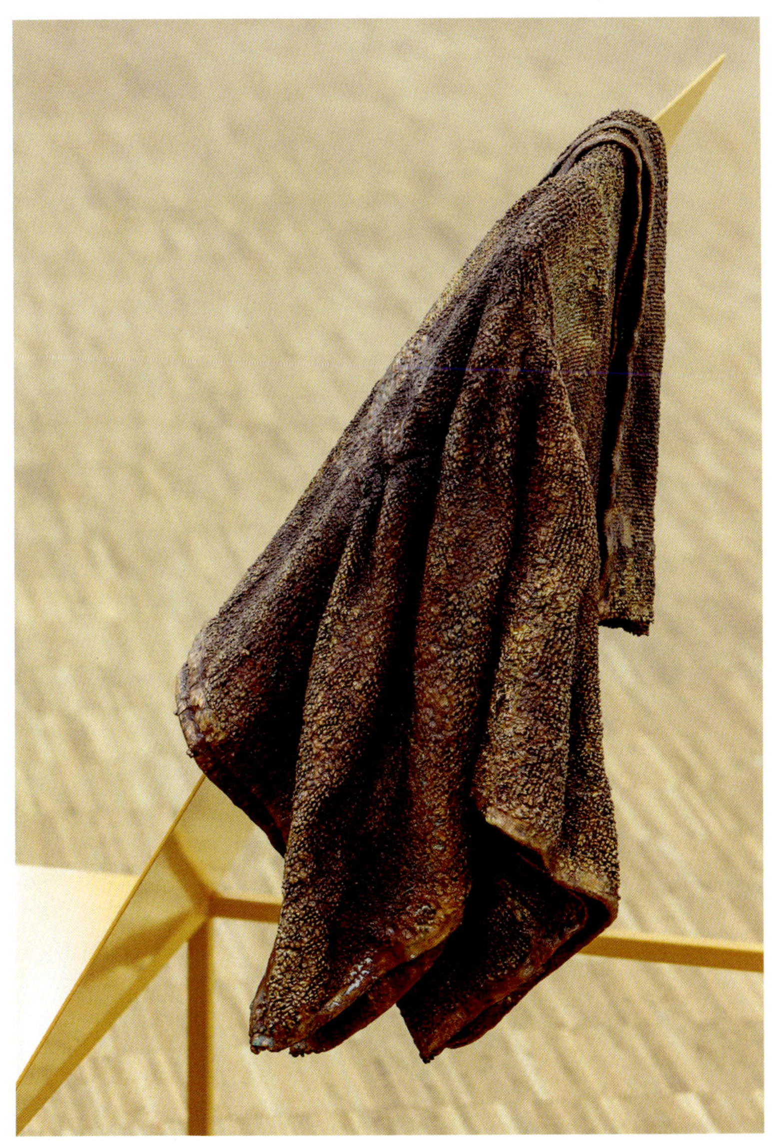

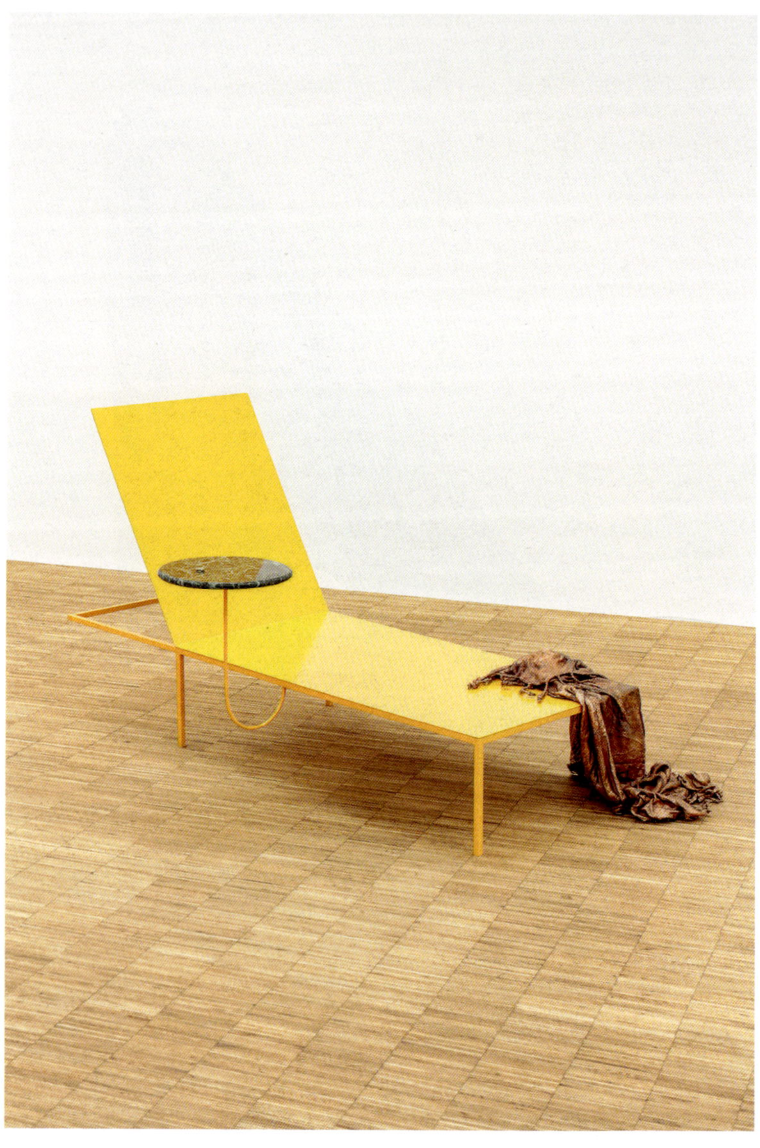

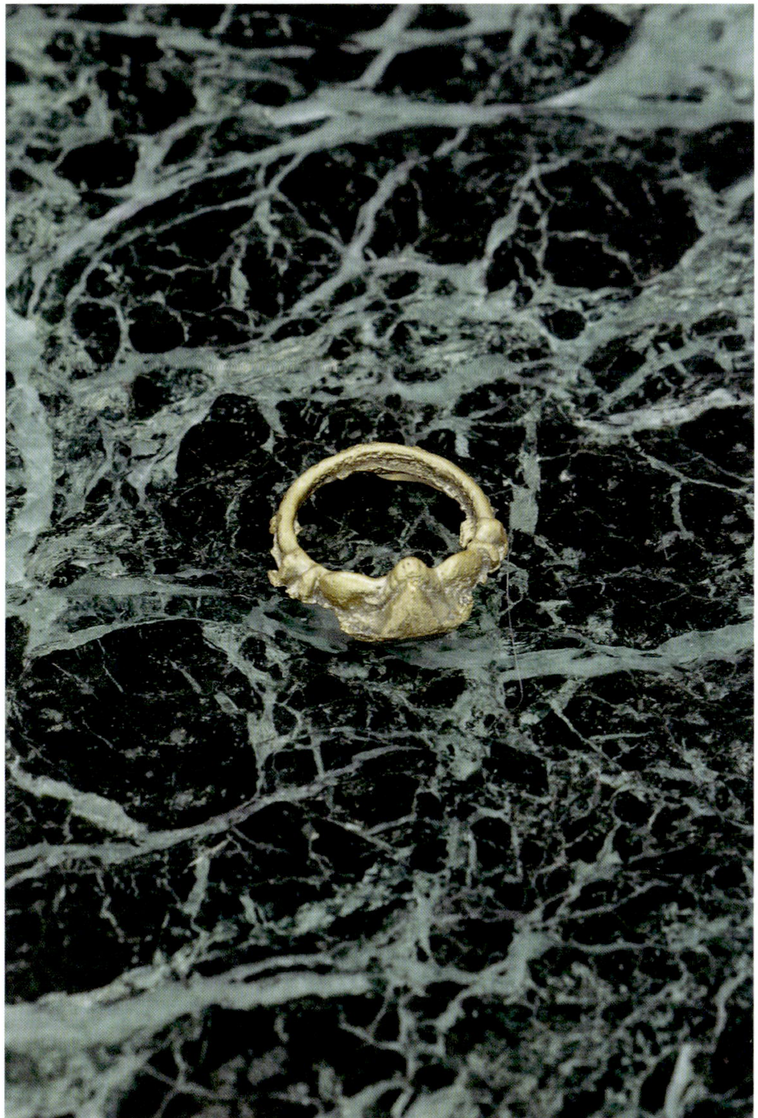

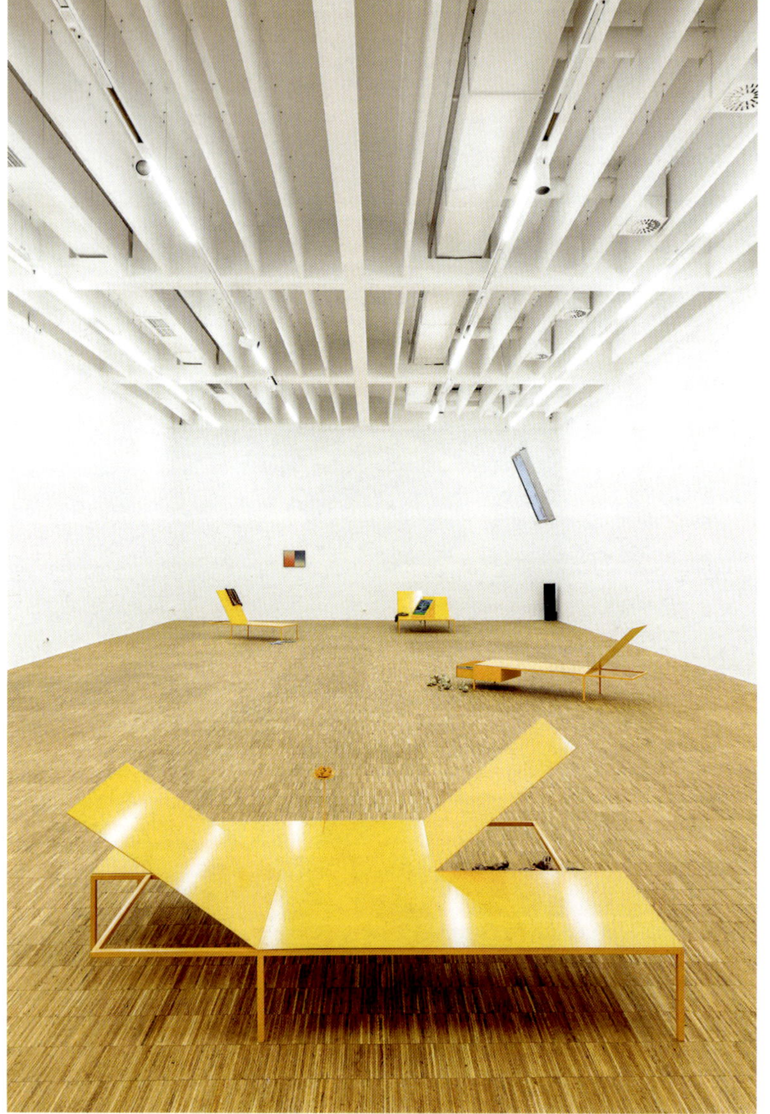

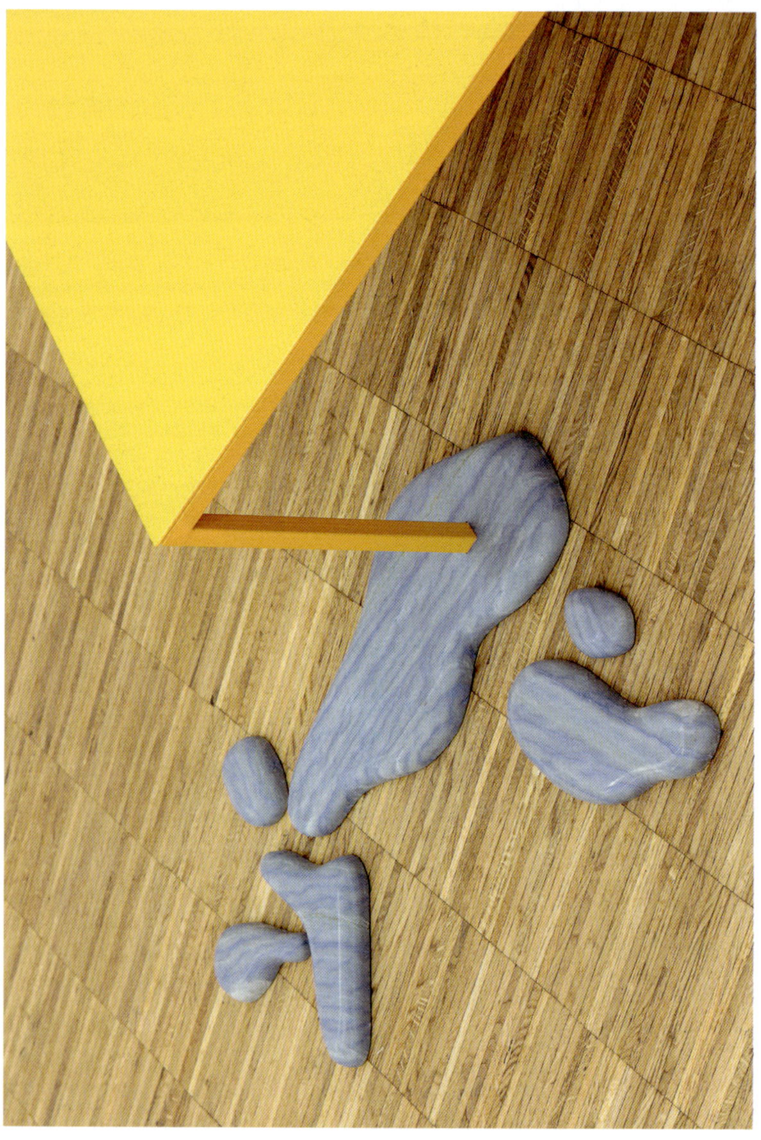

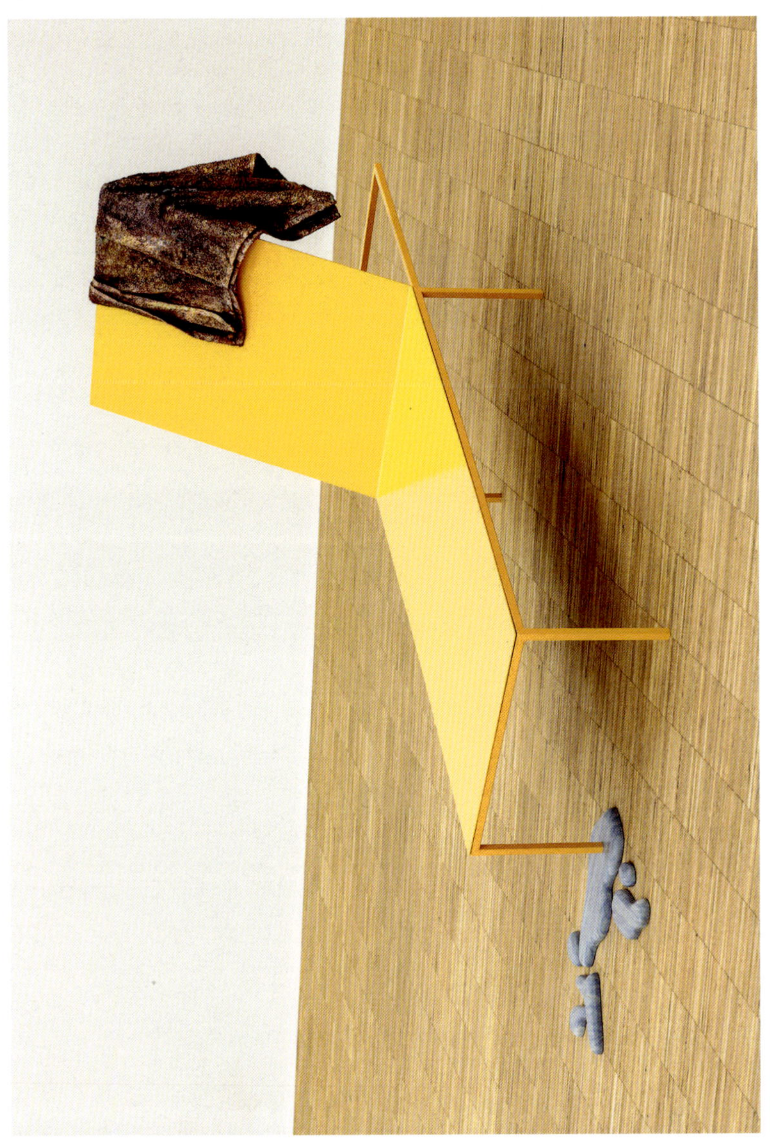

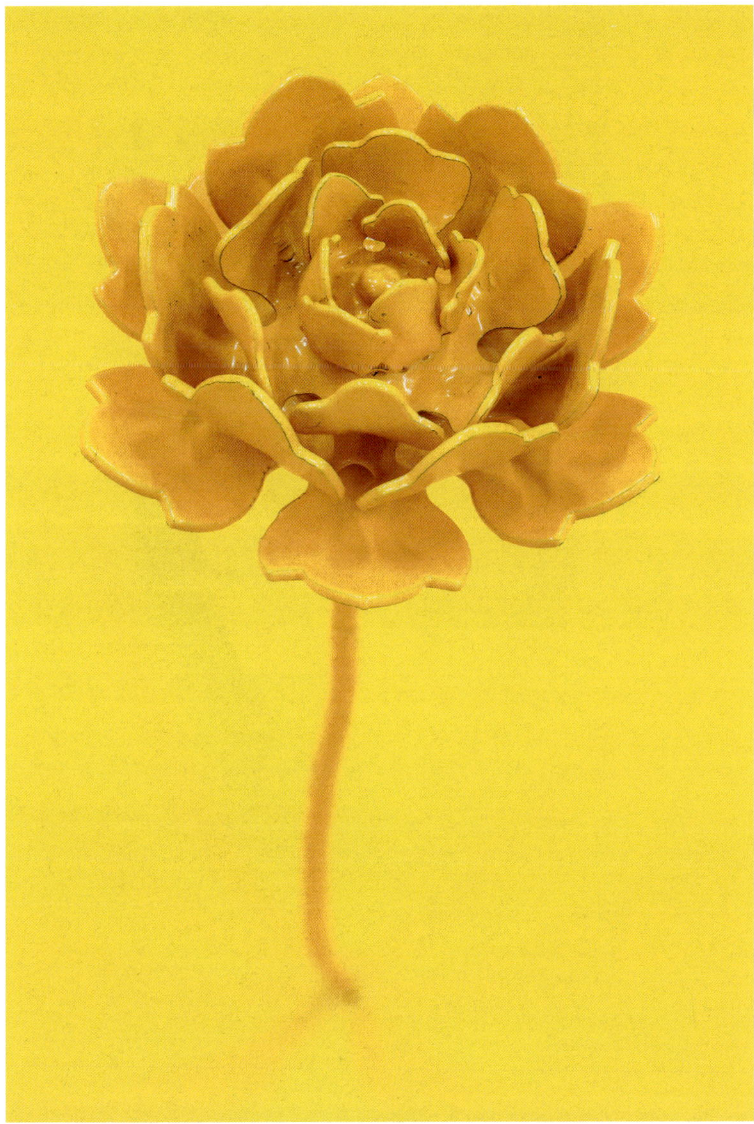

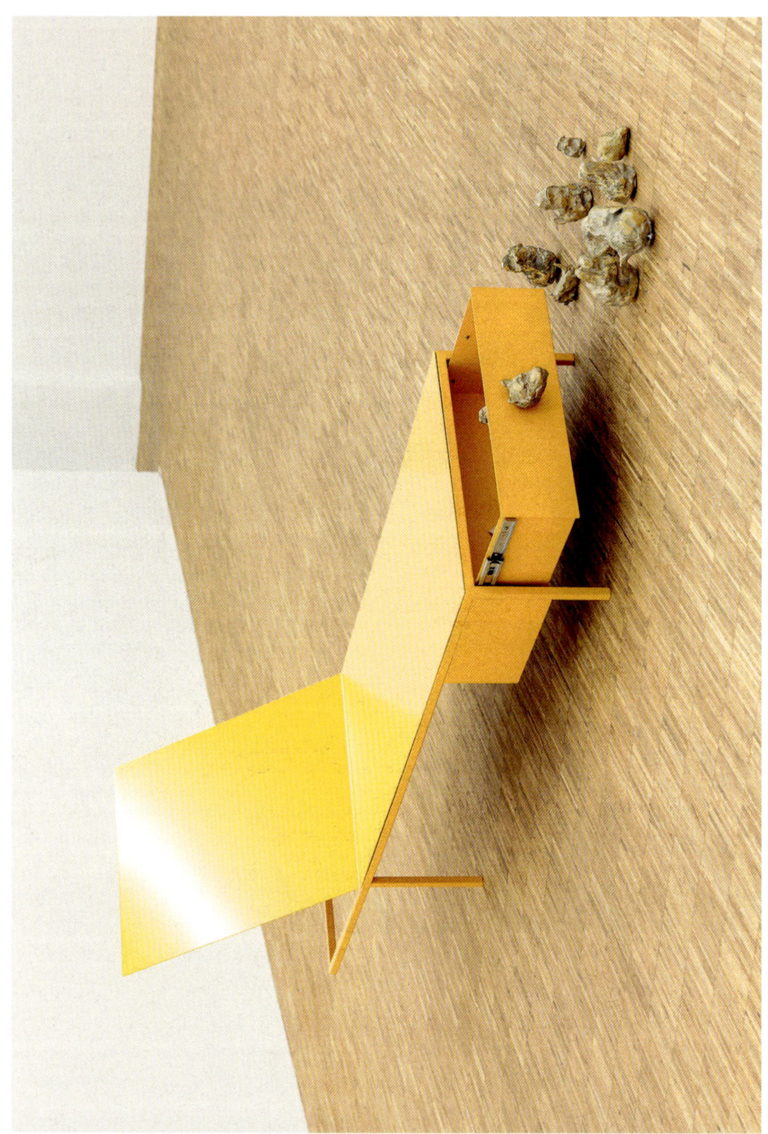

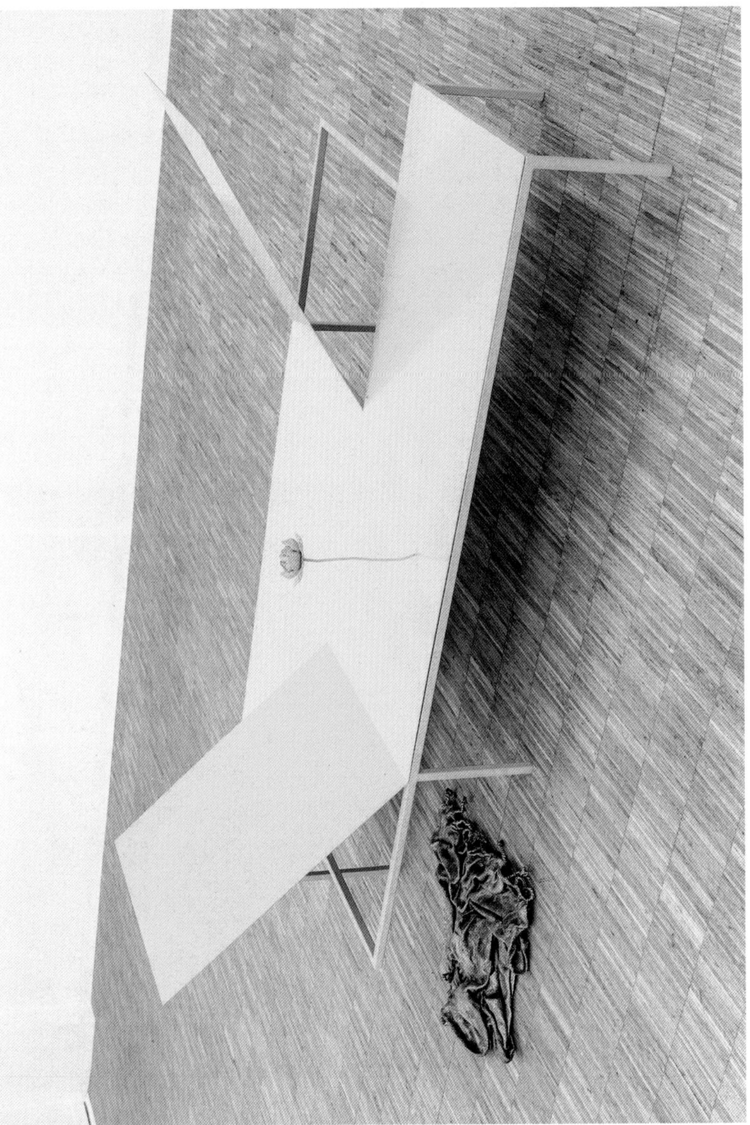

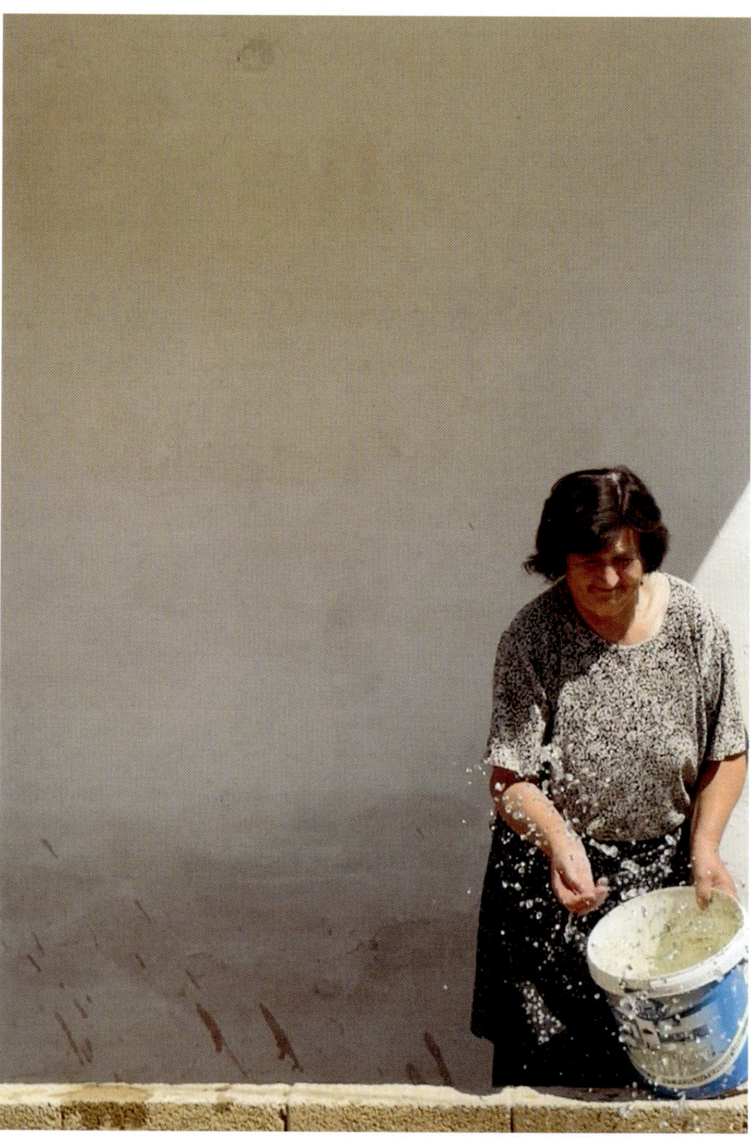

Η ΚΑΘΗΜΕΡΙΝΗ

Ημερήσια Πολιτική και Οικονομική Εφημερίδα

: Γ. Α. Βλάχος   ΑΘΗΝΑ, ΤΕΤΑΡΤΗ 25 ΟΚΤΩΒΡΙΟΥ 2023   1,20

Διάλυση σε ζωντανή ...ση

ε όρους ριάλιτι ο εμφύλιος «προεδρικών» και εσωκομματικής ...ΣΥΡΙΖΑ

κό διάλυσης σε ζωντανή μετάδοση, ς η ανταλλαγή πυρών μεταξύ «προε- ν» και εσωκομματικής αντιπολίτευ- ίνεται από τις τηλεοράσεις και τα φωνα, επικρατεί στον ΣΥΡΙΖΑ στον κο της επιλογής του Στέφανου Κασ- ν να δείξει την πόρτα της εξόδου

στους Νίκο Φίλη, Πάνο Σκουρλέτη και Δημήτρη Βίτσα. Η επιλογή του προέδρου του ΣΥΡΙΖΑ προκάλεσε την πικρή αντίδραση των Έφης Αχτσιόγλου, Νάσου Ηλιόπουλου και Αλέξη Χαρίτση, που έκαναν λόγο για «κατήφορο», ενώ ο Ευκλείδης Τσακαλώτος αναφέρθηκε σε «αποκεφαλισμό», με

την πλευρά της ηγεσίας να αντεπιτι αναφερόμενη σε «κατασυκοφάντηση κ υπονόμευση». Εάν η διάσπαση του ΣΥΡΙ- ΖΑ, που πλέον θεωρείται αναπόφευκτη, δεν συντελεστεί άμεσα, «μητέρα των μαχών» θα αποτελέσει η προγραμματισμένη για τις 11 και 12 Νοεμβρίου Κεντρική

ρικοί» αναφέρουν ...μοί στην Κ.Ε. τους ευ- ...εάν οι συνθήκες το επιτρέ- ψουν είναι ανοικτό από την πλευρά της εσωκομματικής αντιπολίτευσης να τεθεί ζήτημα λειτουργίας του κόμματος ή ακόμη και ηγεσίας. Σελ. 3, 4

«Κάποια μέρα θα ξαναγυρίσουμε στα άστρα»

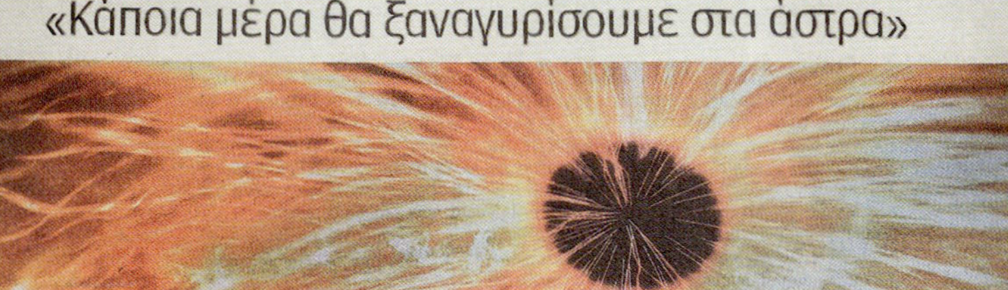

Νέου τύπου αντικειμενικά κριτήρια διαβίωσης

Για ελεύθερους επαγγελματίες

Νέας γενιάς αντικειμενικά κριτήρια διαβίωσης επεξεργάζεται το υπουργείο Οικονομικών για τους ελεύθε-

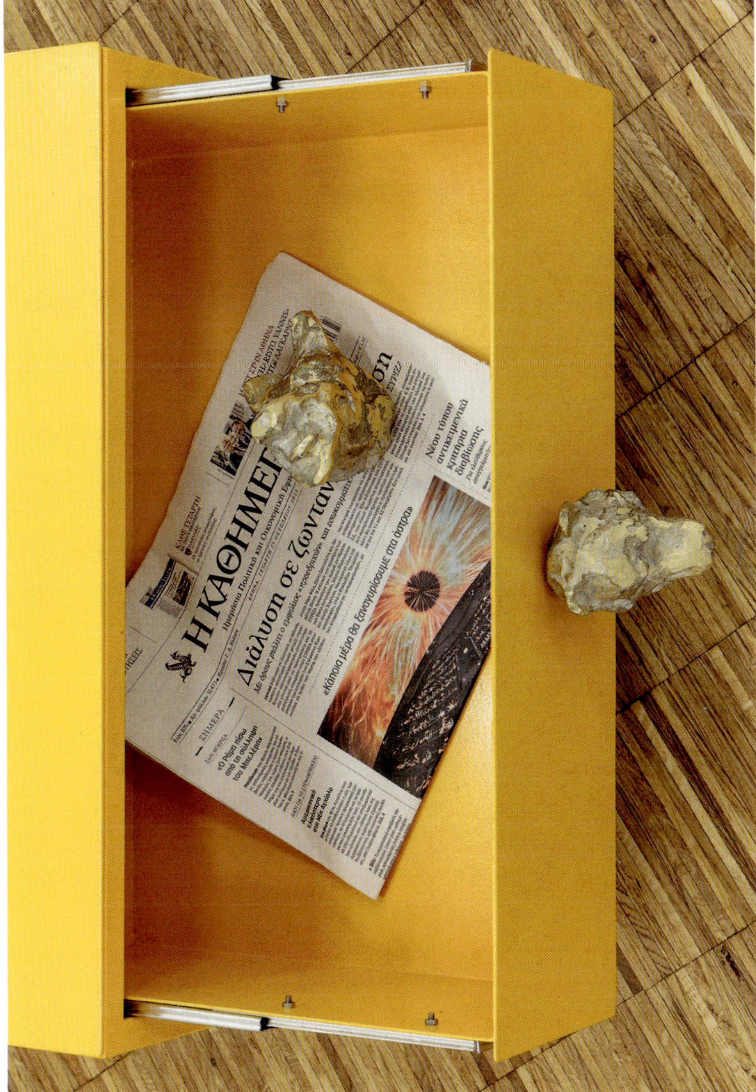

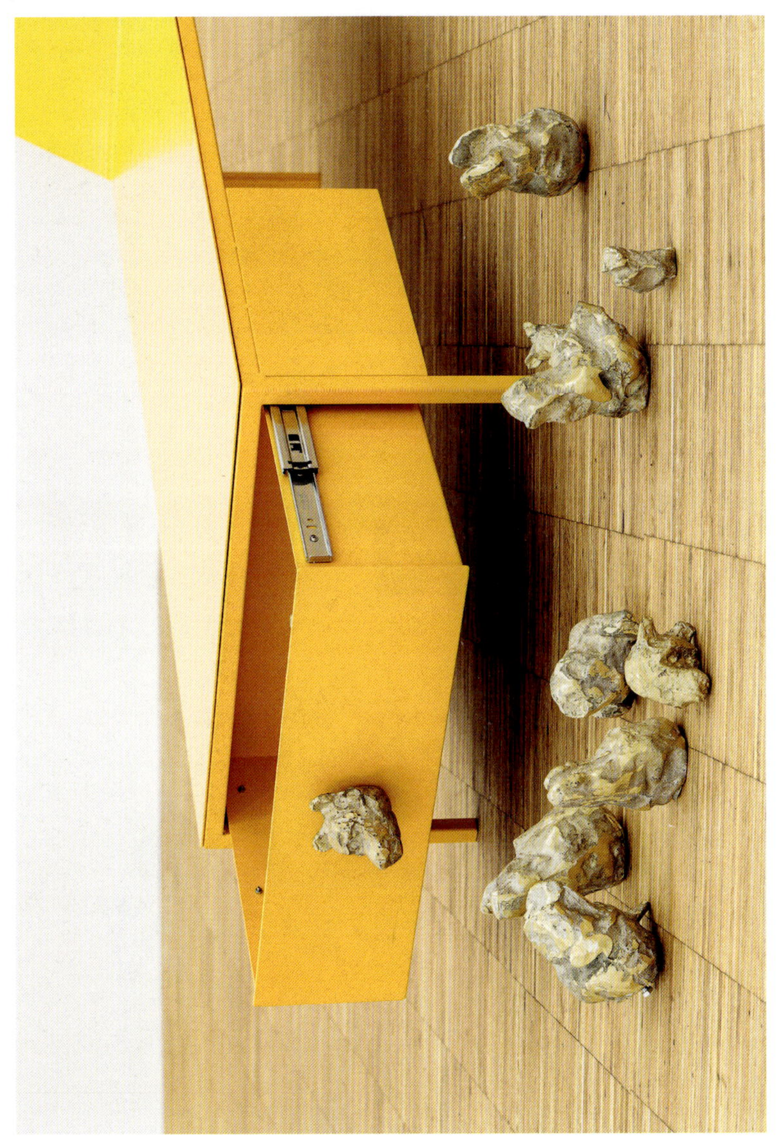

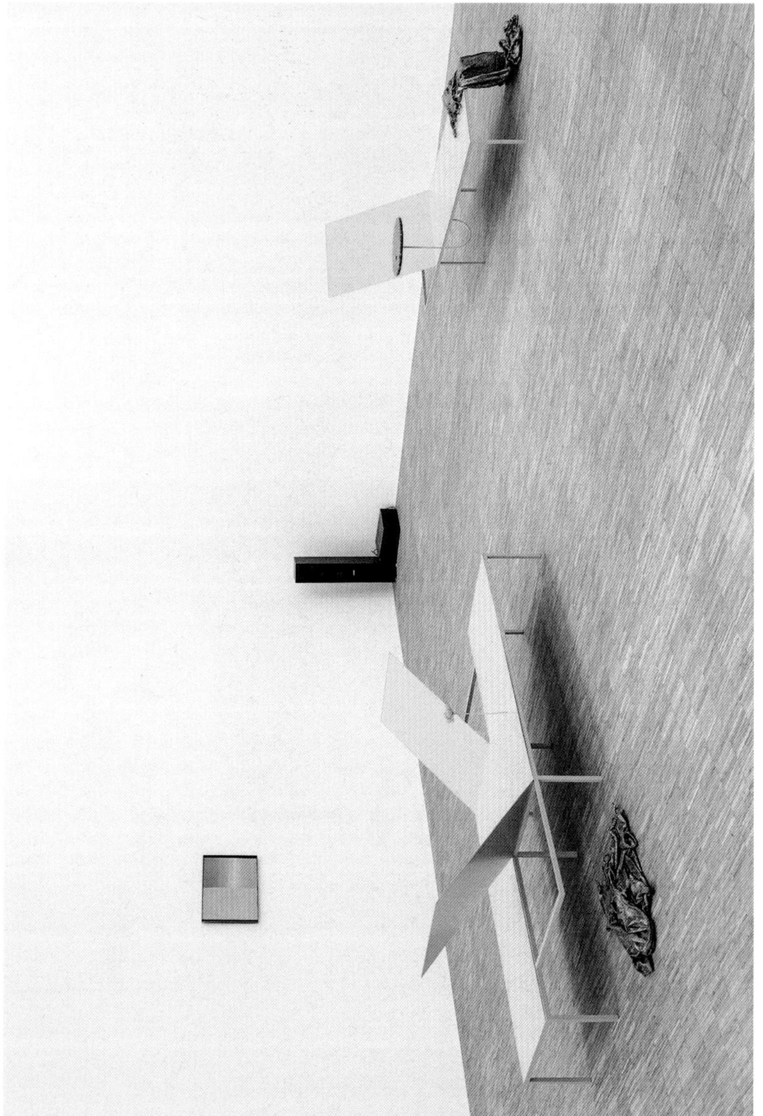

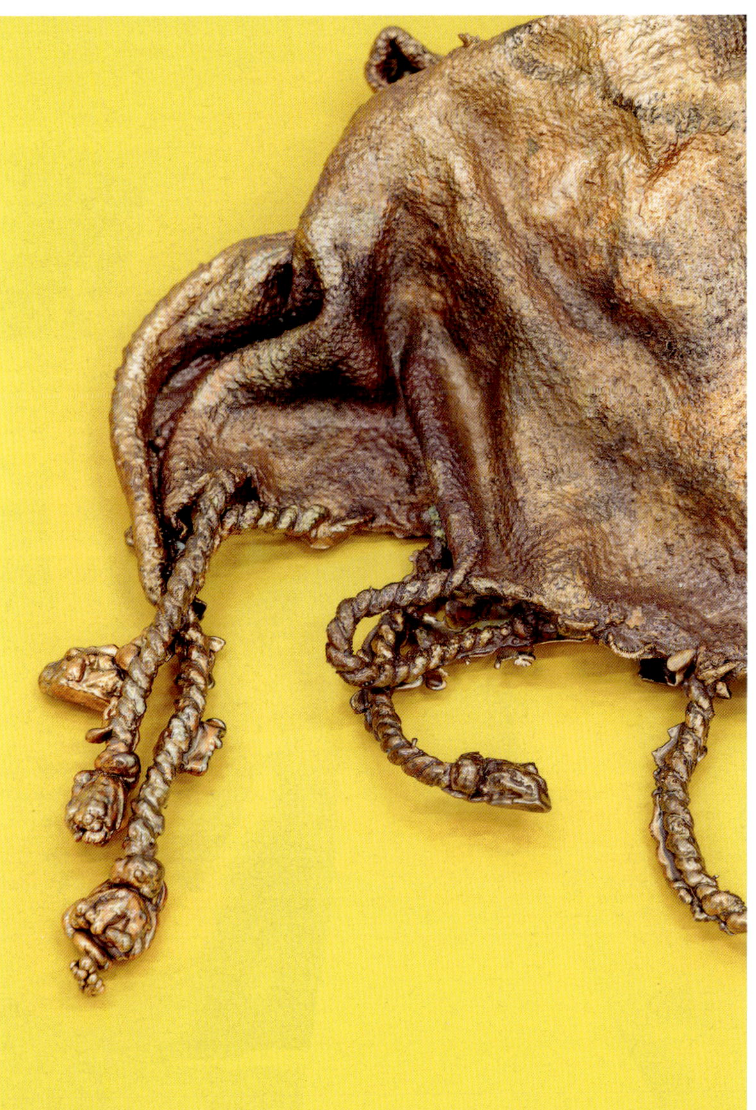

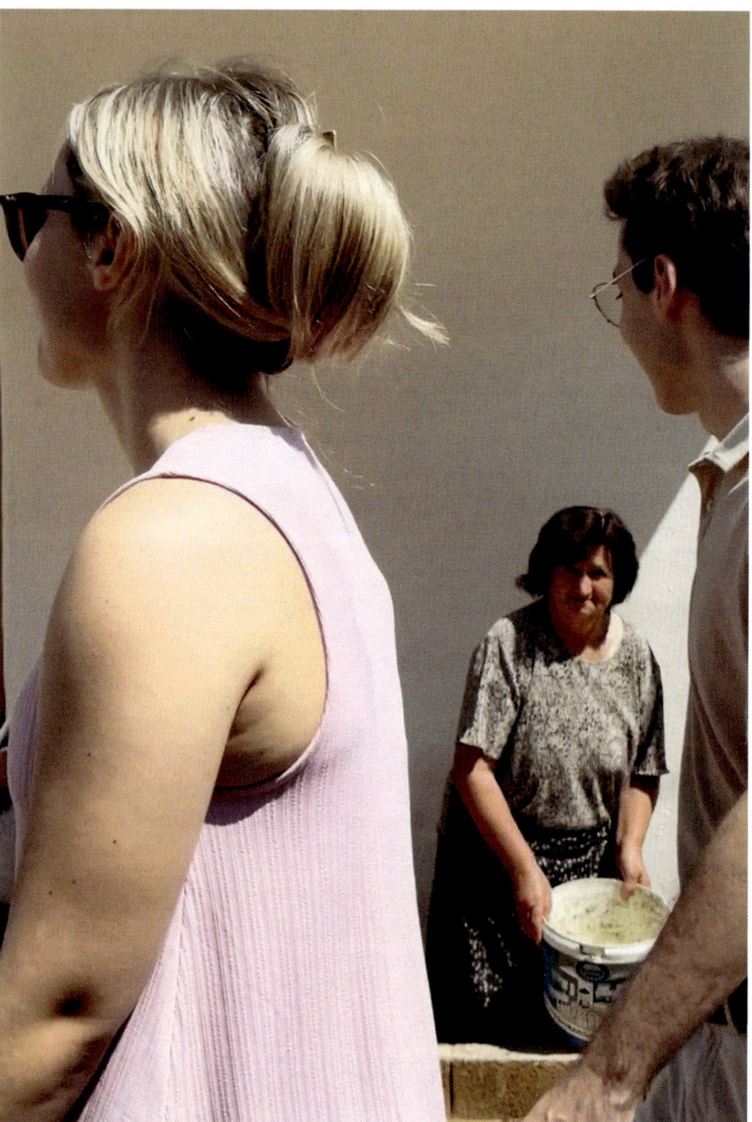

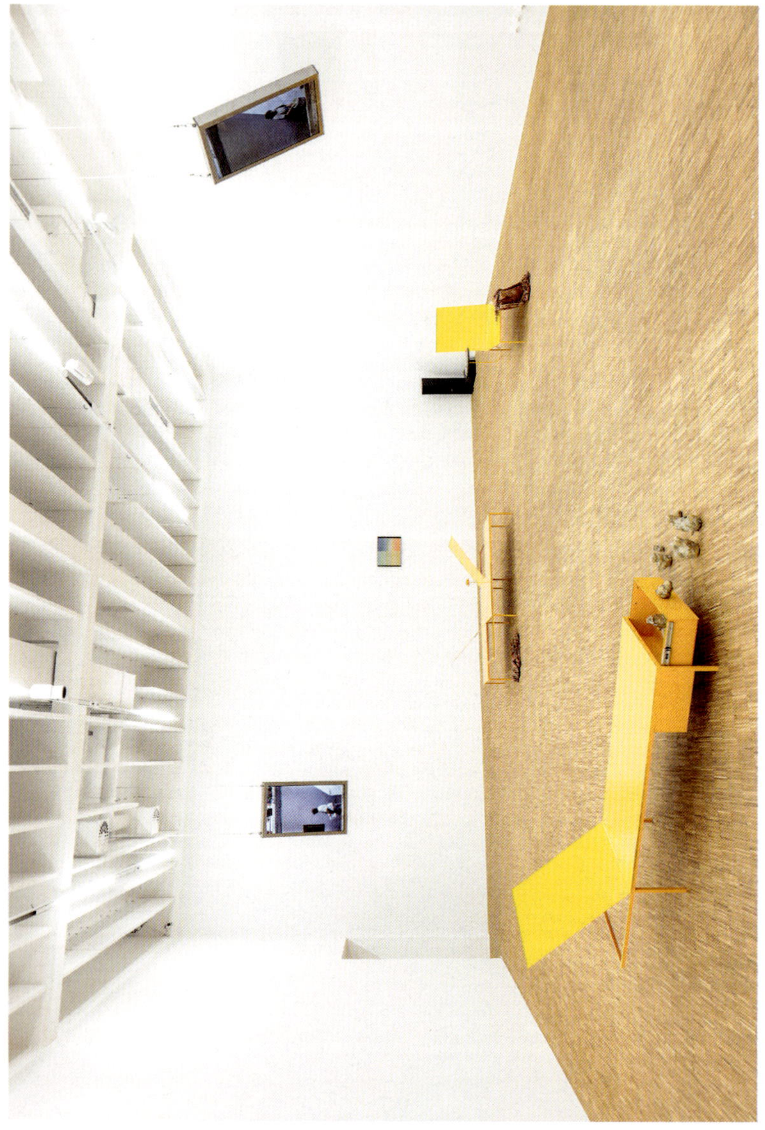

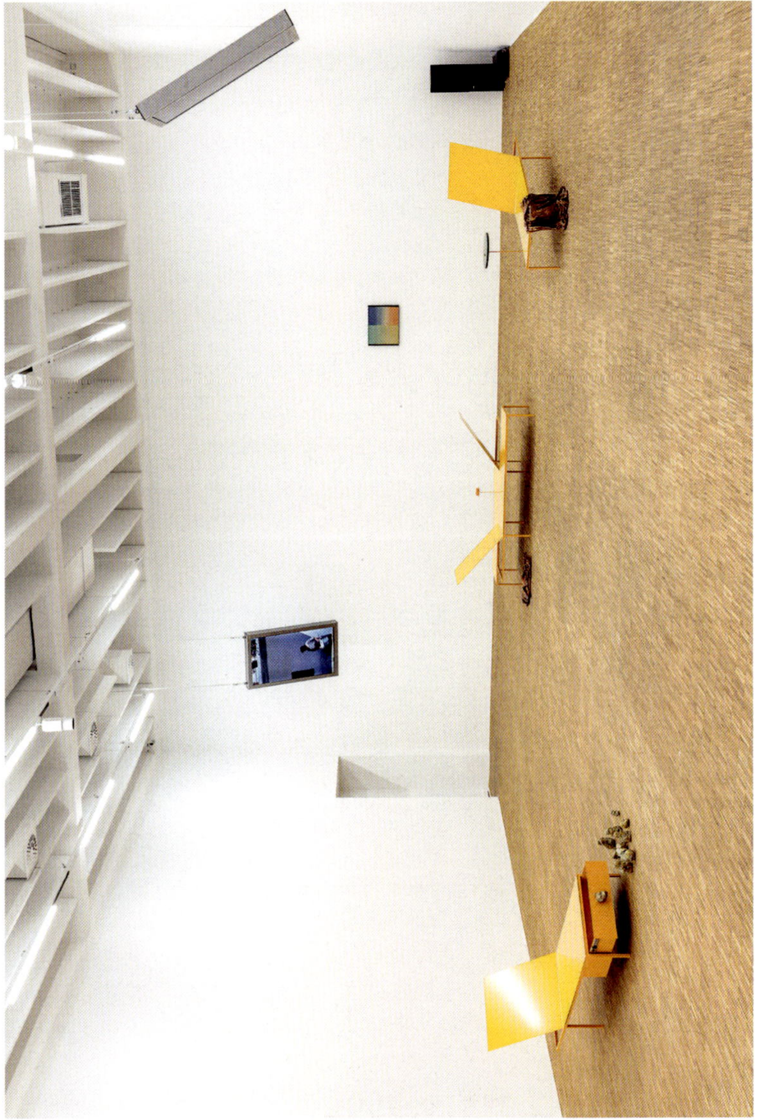

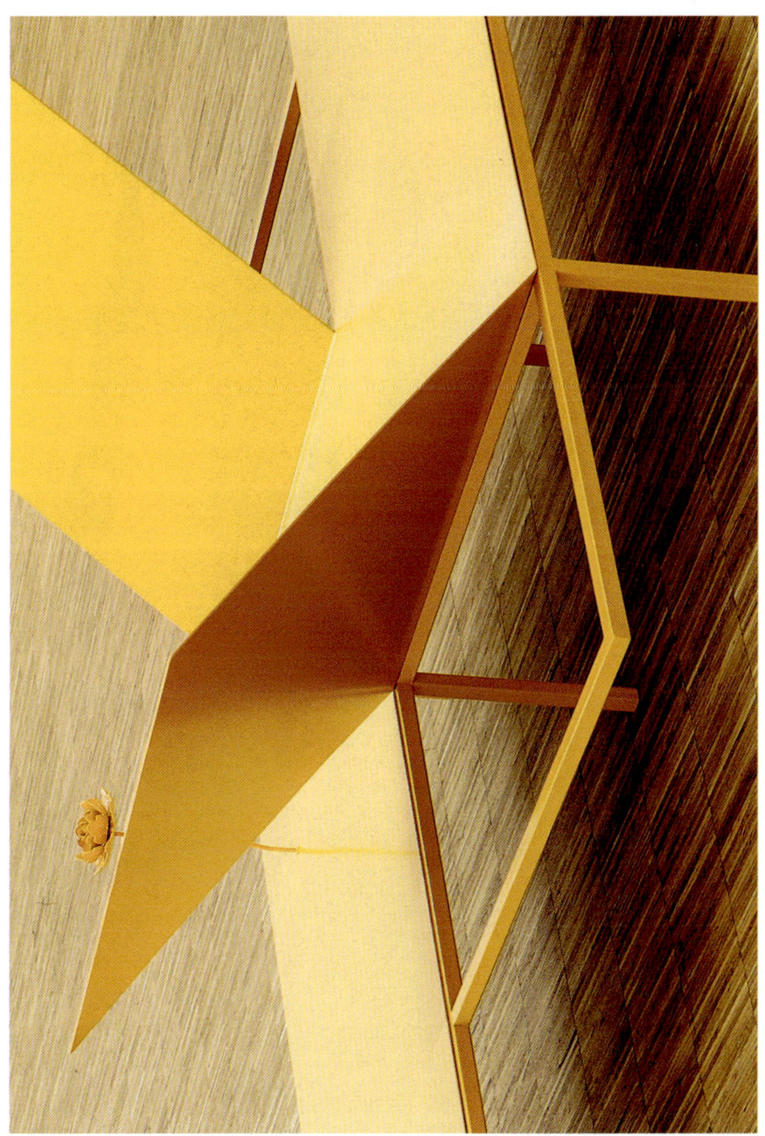

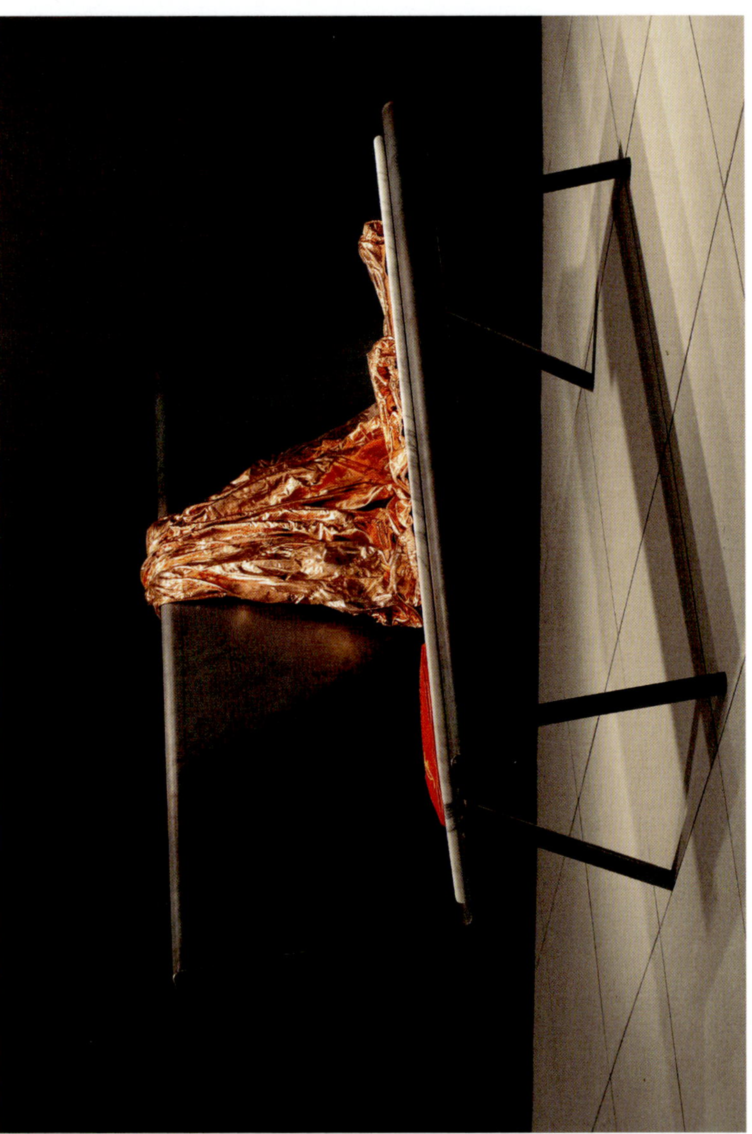

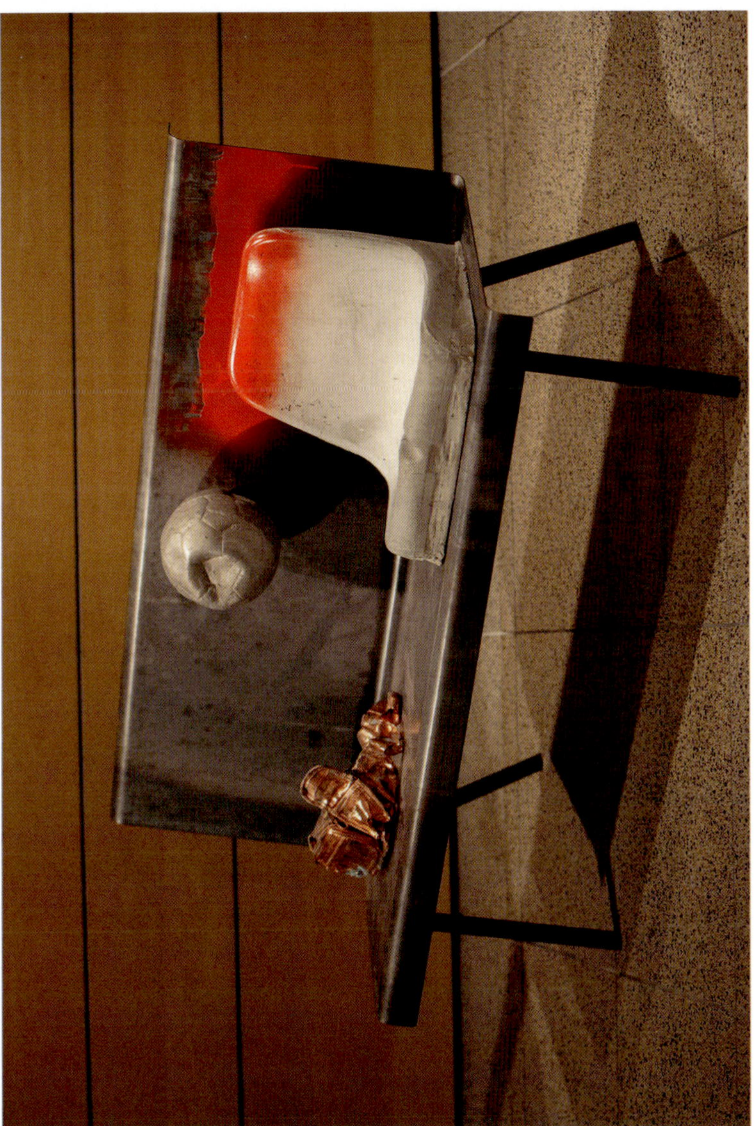

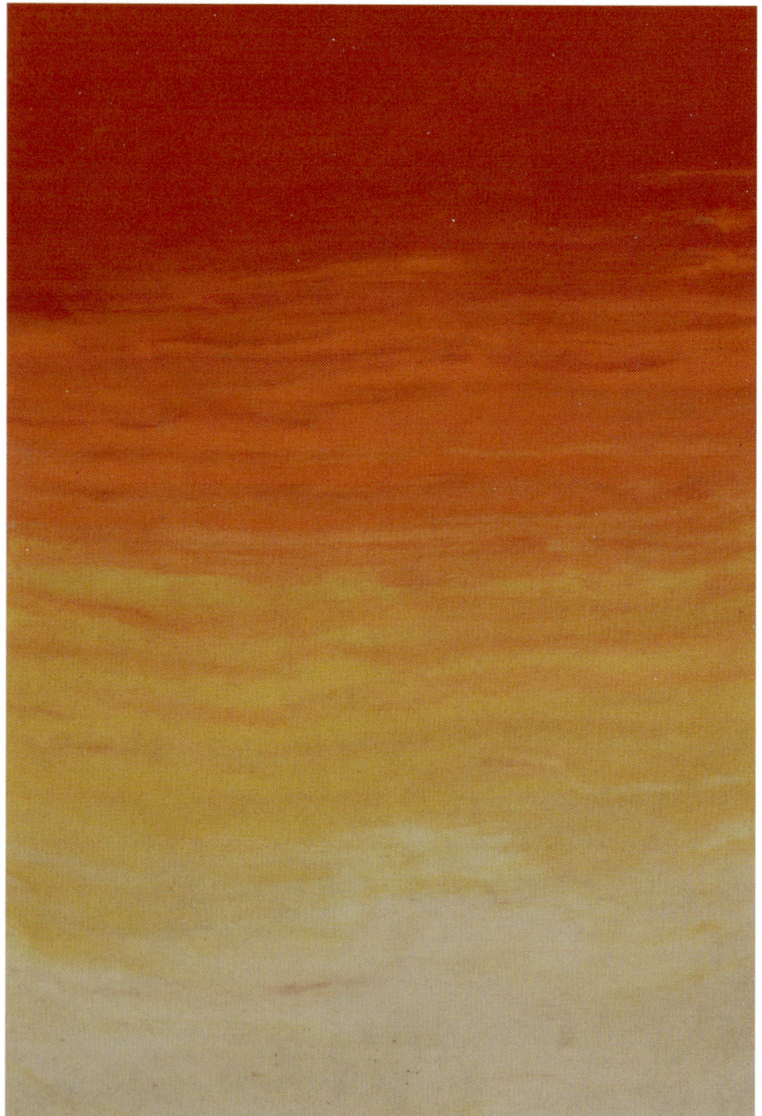

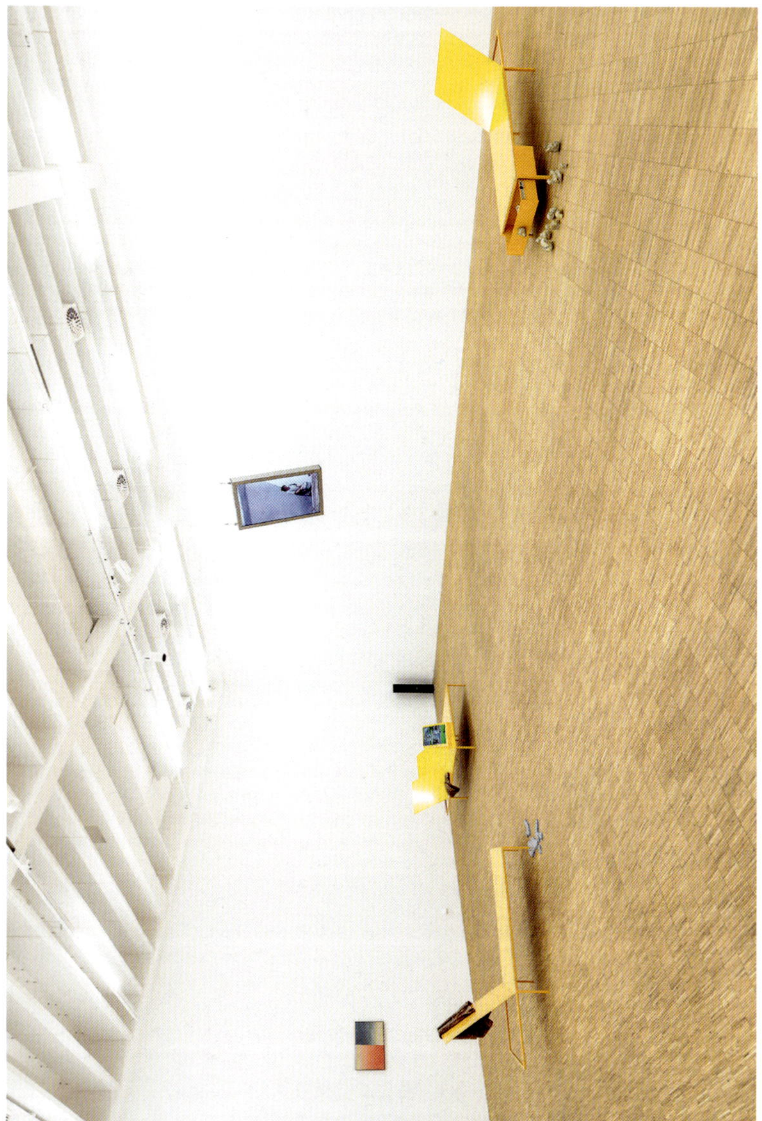

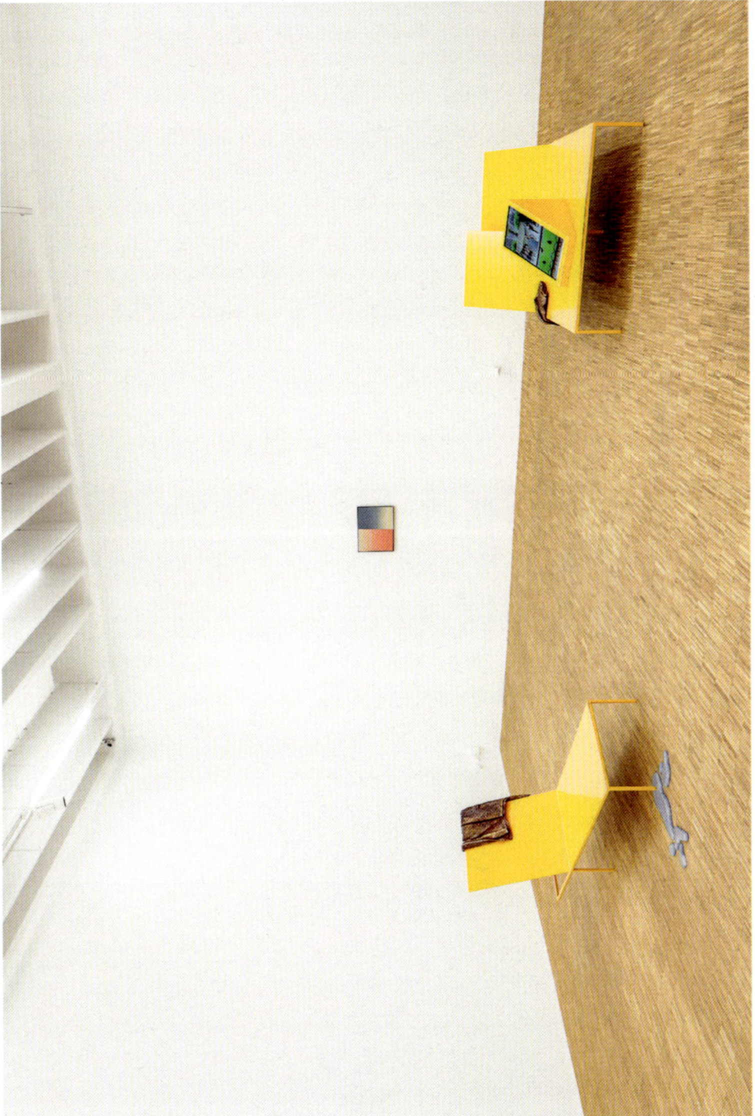

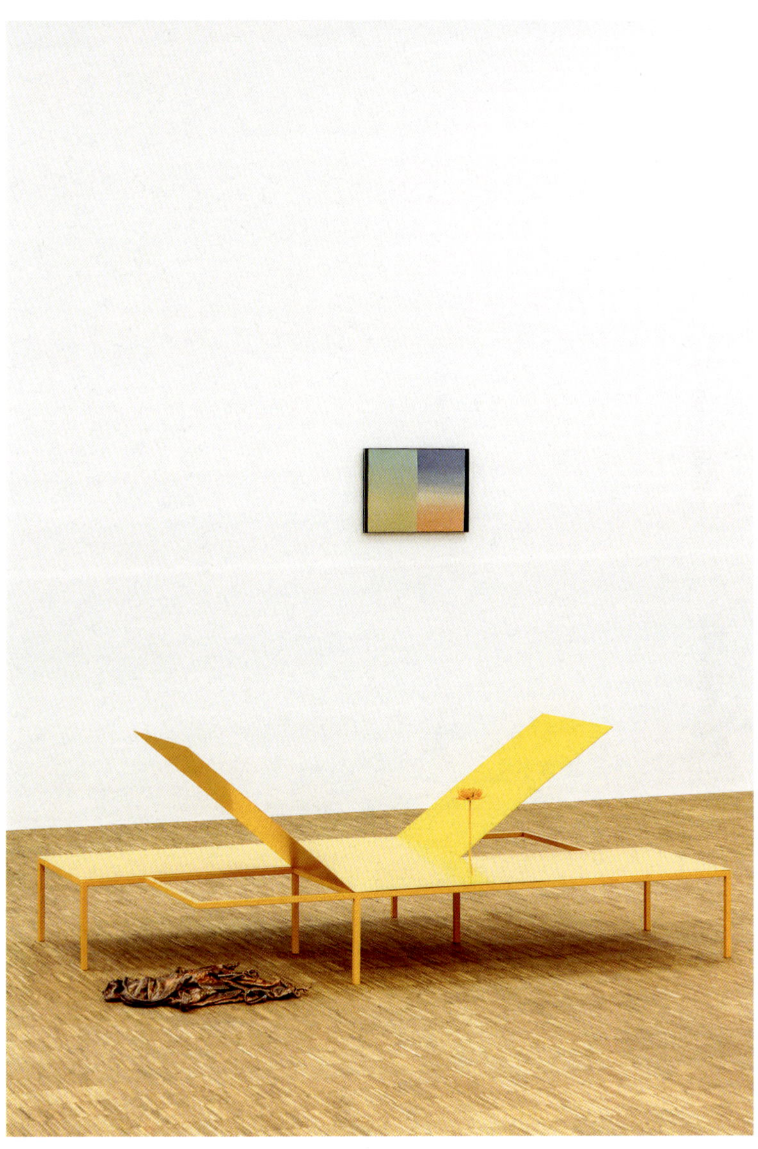

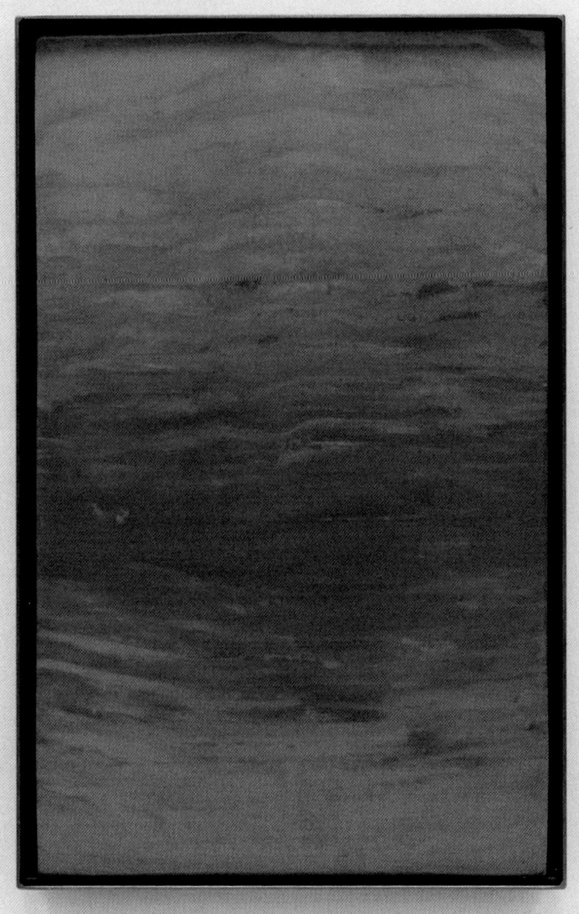

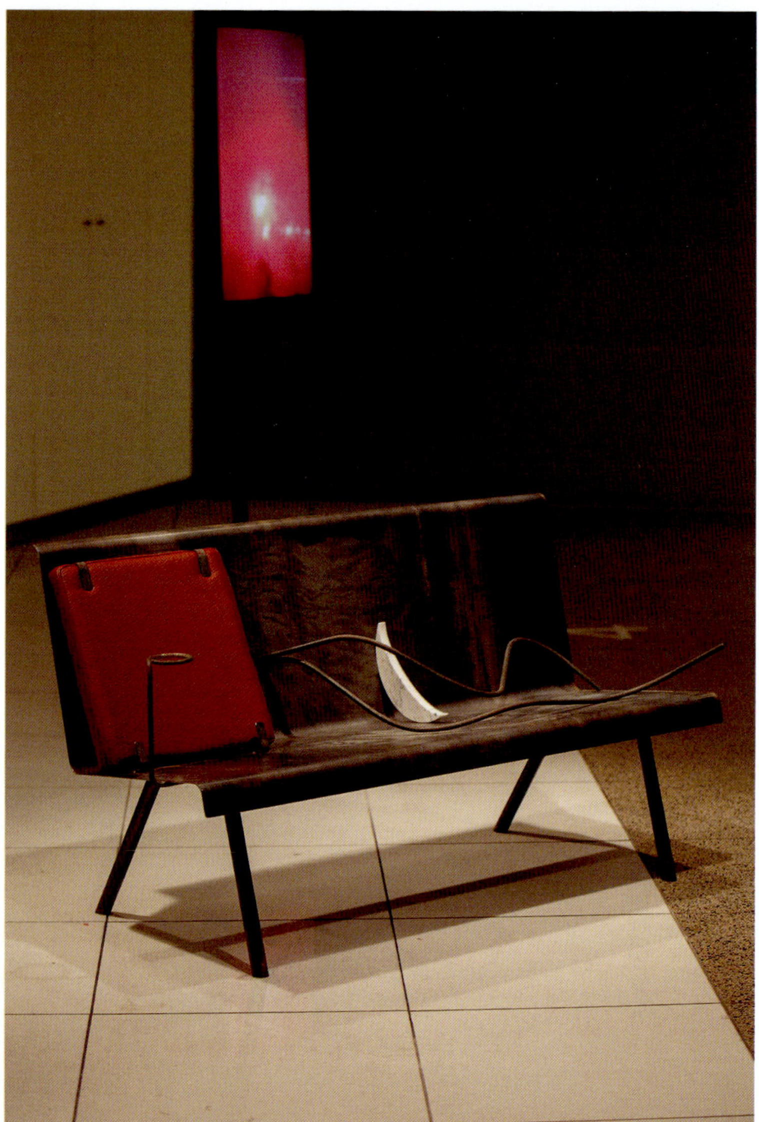

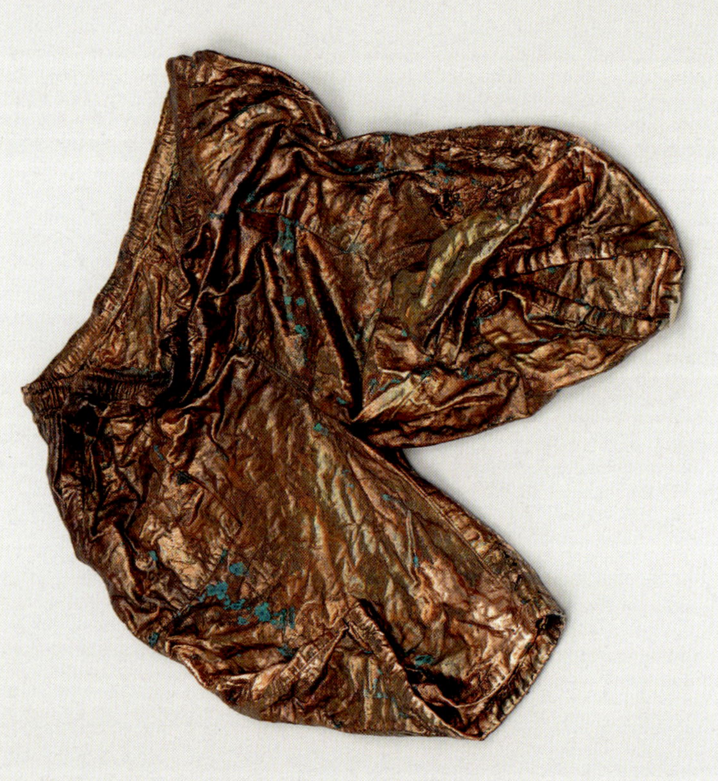

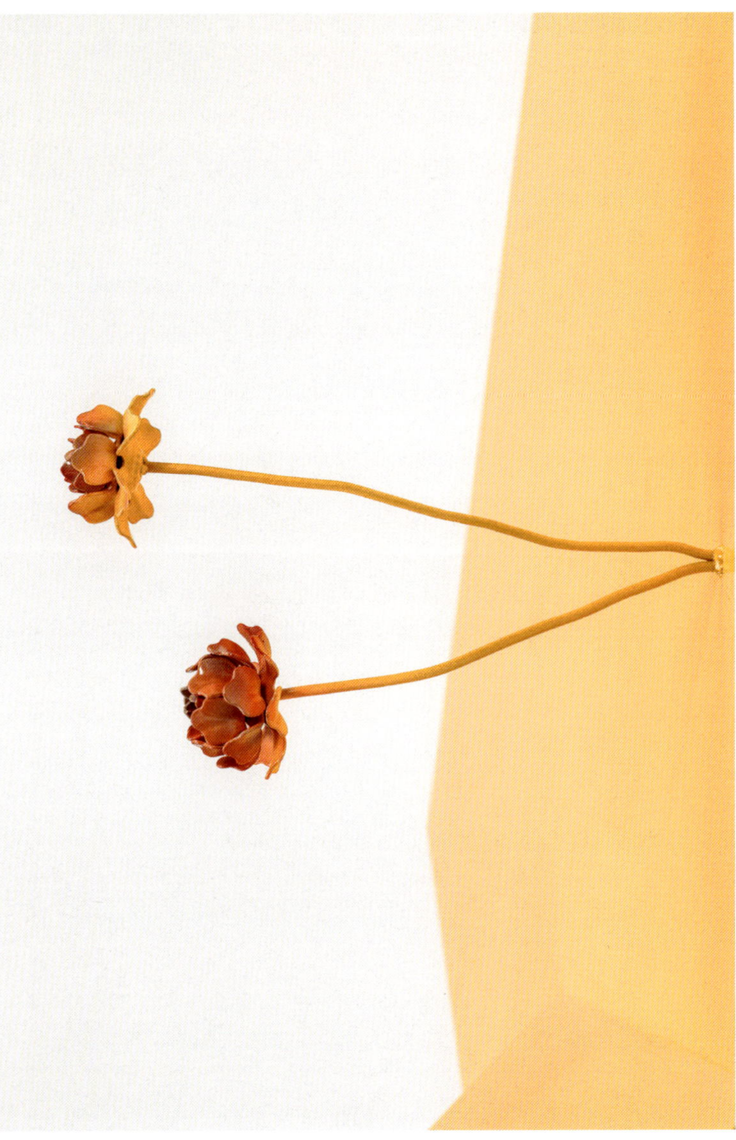

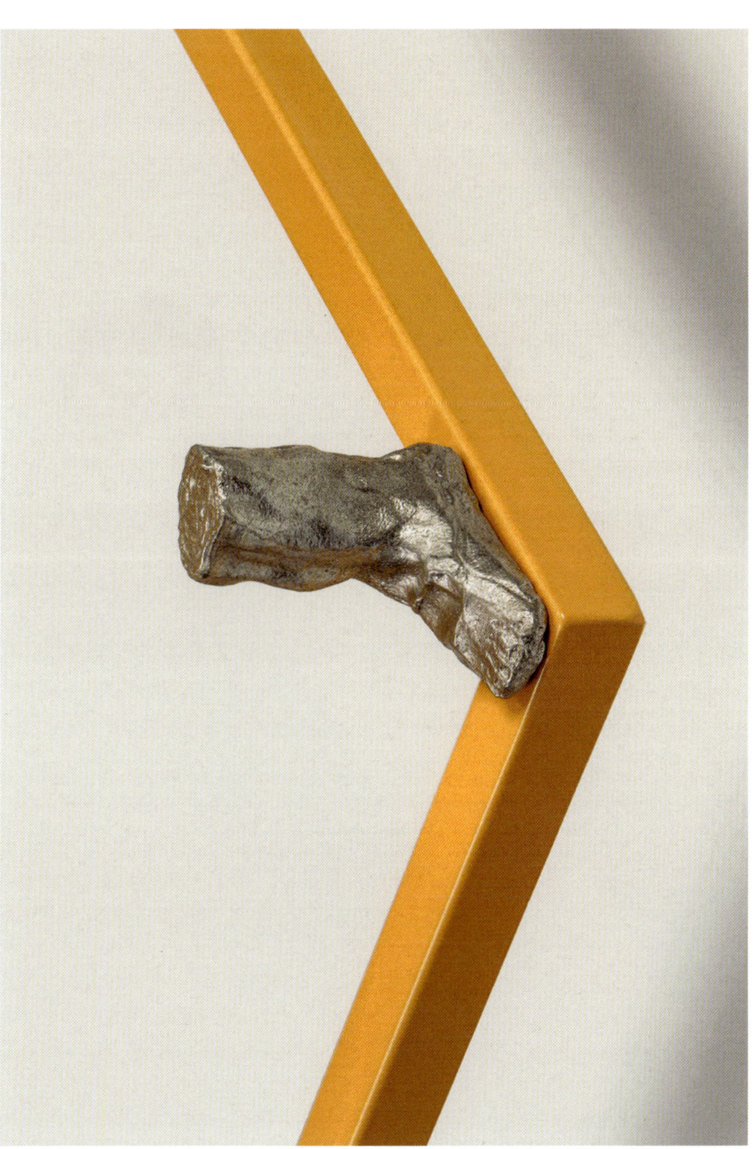

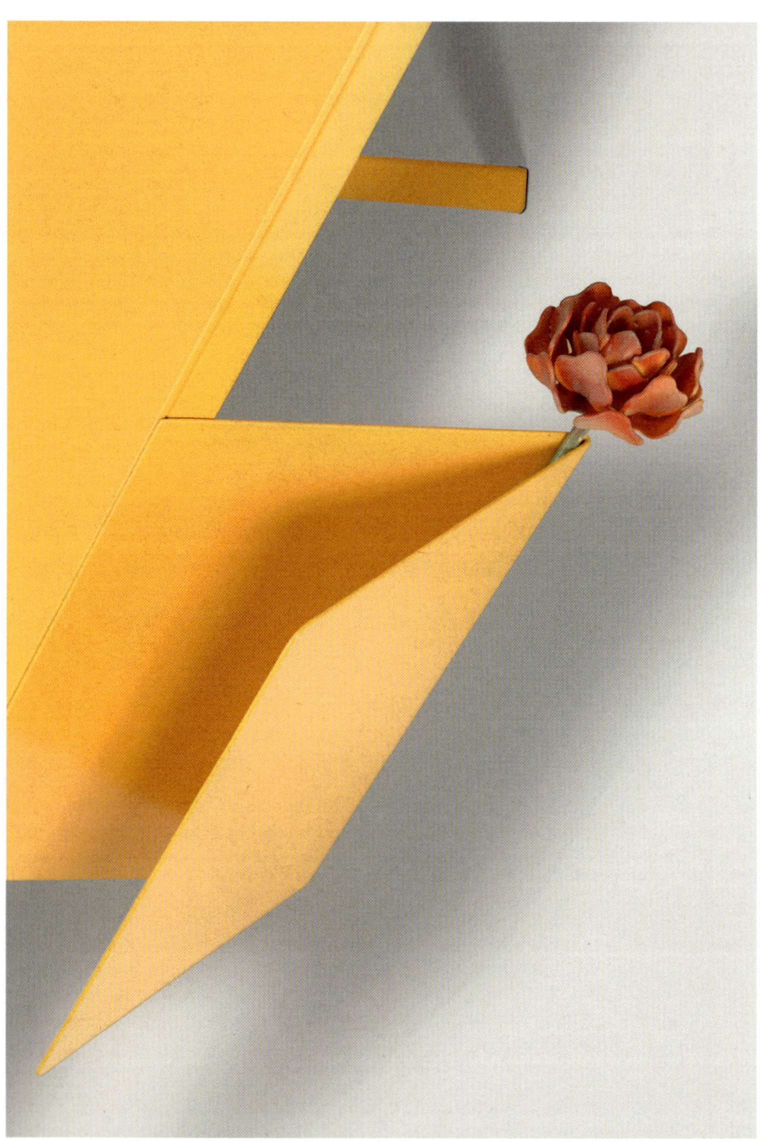

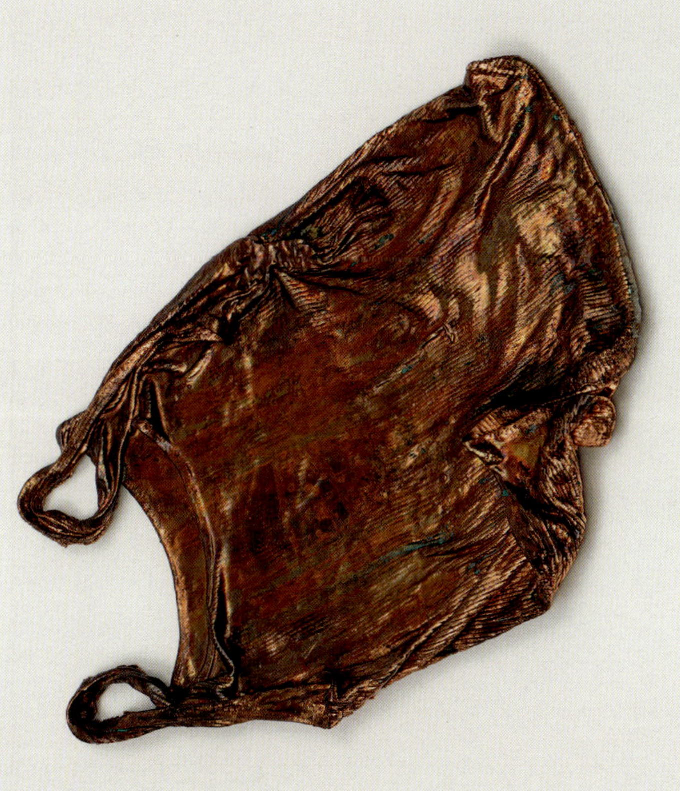

LIST OF WORKS

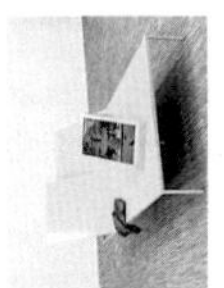

65, 66, 70, 71

Sunbed V (Double), 2024, painted steel, video, screen, copper plated beach towel, 178 × 120 × 85 cm

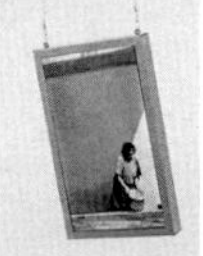

67, 72, 88, 96

May They Go Like Water, and Flow Back to Us, 2024, digital video, 12 sec., edition 1 of 3

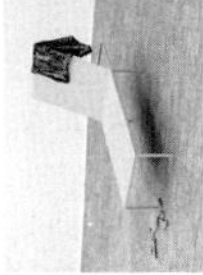

77, 82, 83

Sunbed II, 2024, painted steel, Macauba marble, copper plated beach towel, 170 × 70 × 99 cm

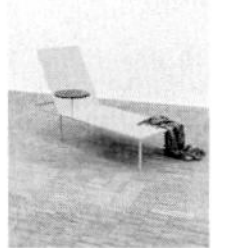

78, 79, 95

Sunbed I, 2024, painted steel, copper plated beach towel Tinos marble, cast bronze ring, 193 × 95 × 96 cm

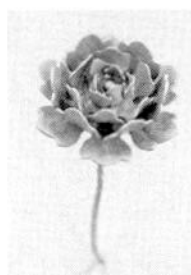

85, 101

Sunbed IV (Double), 2024, painted steel, 213 × 120 × 82 cm, detail

86, 90, 91, 93

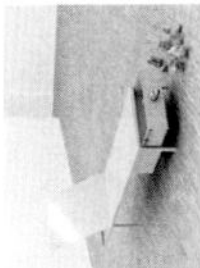

Sunbed III, 2024, painted steel, newspaper, cast bronze, 209 × 60 × 84 cm

87

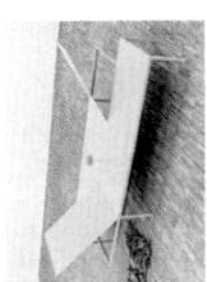

Sunbed IV (Double), 2024, painted steel, 213 × 120 × 82 cm. On the floor: *Beach Towel I*, 2024, copper plated beach towel, 67 × 67 × 67 cm

94

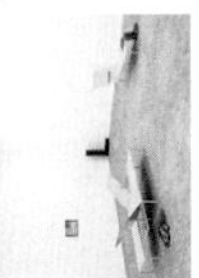

Front left: *Sunbed IV (Double)*, 2024, painted steel, 213 × 120 × 82 cm. Front right: *Sunbed I*, 2024, painted steel, copper plated beach towel Tinos marble, cast bronze ring, 193 × 95 × 96 cm. On the wall: *07:28 to 18:55*, 2023, ceramic, steel, 56 × 42 × 1.4 cm. In the corner: *Op. 1 (with Dimitris Prokos)*, 2024, sound, 7 hrs., edition 1 of 3

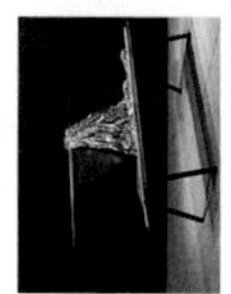

102

Together We Don't Stand (I), 2021, steel, copper plated fabric, marble, embroidered leatherette pillow, 140 × 80 × 85 cm

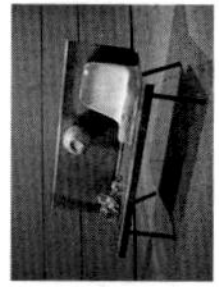

103

Together We Don't Stand (III), 2021, steel, copper plated fabric, cement, cast aluminium and spray paint, 140 × 80 × 85 cm

104

20:39, 2024, ceramic, steel, 42 × 26.8 × 2 cm

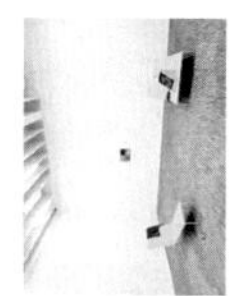

107

Front: *Sunbed II*, 2024, painted steel, Macauba marble, copper plated beach towel, 170 × 70 × 99 cm. Front right: *Sunbed V (Double)*, 2024, painted steel, video, screen, copper plated beach towel, 178 × 120 × 85 cm. On the wall: *07:17 to 19:13*, 2023, ceramic, steel, 56 × 42 × 1.4 cm

109

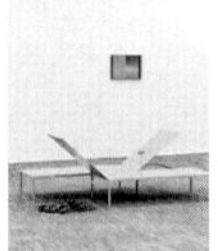

Front: *Sunbed IV (Double)*, 2024, painted steel, 213 × 120 × 82cm. On the floor: *Beach Towel I*, 2024, copper plated beach towel, 67 × 67 × 67 cm. On the wall: *07:28 to 18:55*, 2023, ceramic, steel, 56 × 42 × 1.4 cm

110

20:44, 2024, ceramic, steel, 42 × 26.8 × 2 cm

111

20:01, 2024, ceramic, steel, 42 × 26.8 × 2 cm

112

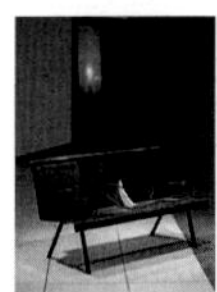

Together We Don't Stand (II), 2021, steel, marble, leatherette pillow, 140 × 80 × 85 cm

114

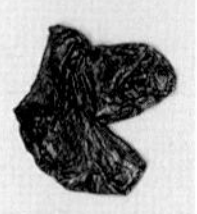

Shorts, 2024, copper plated shorts, 50 × 53 × 4 cm

115, 117

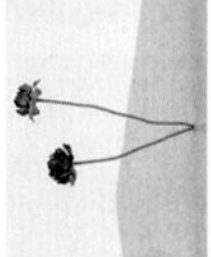

Sunbed VI, 2024, painted steel, cast aluminium, 188 × 165 × 82 cm, detail

118

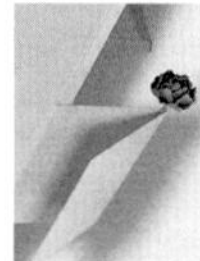

Sunbed VIII, 2024, painted steel, cast bronze rings, 173 × 123 × 86 cm, detail

119

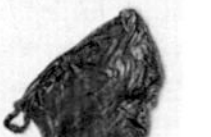

Tank Top, 2024, copper plated tank top, 54 × 34 × 4 cm

121

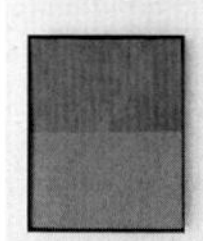

06:35 to 18:32, 2024, ceramic, steel, 52.5 × 41.7 × 2 cm

24–29, 54–61

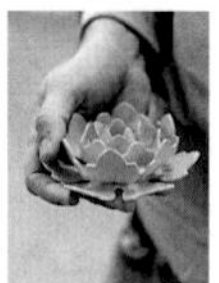

Vasilis's Papageorgiou studio views. Courtesy of the artist

CREDITS

All works: Courtesy of the artist

46, 47, 48, 49, 50, 51, 52, 53, 54, 55, 56, 57, 58, 59, 60, 61
Photo: Alina Lefa

65–67, 69–71, 74–75, 77–80, 82–83, 85–87, 90–91, 93–95, 98–99, 101, 106–107, 109
Exhibition view Vasilis Papageorgiou, *Sunseekers or Dimming the Sun or*, Salzburger Kunstverein 2024.
Photo: kunst-dokumentation

102–103, 112
Exhibition view 7th Athens Biennale: Eclipse, commissioned and produced by Athens Biennale.
Photo: Nyssos Vasilopoulos

104, 110–111, 114–115, 117–119, 121
Photo: Stathis Mamalakis

Published by
Mousse Publishing & Salzburger
Kunstverein

Distributed by Mousse Publishing
Contrappunto s.r.l.
Via Pier Candido Decembrio 28,
20137, Milan–Italy

Available through
Mousse Publishing, Milan
moussemagazine.it
salzburgerkunstverein.at

Editor
Mirela Baciak

Publishing editor
Ilaria Bombelli, Mousse

Design
Gloria Favaro, Mousse

Proofreading and copyediting
Emma Passarella, Lindsey Westbrook

Texts by Mirela Baciak,
Julia Morandeira Arrizabalaga,
Petros Phokaides, Danai Giannoglou,
Kostas Stasinopoulos

First edition
2024

Printed in Italy
by Grafiche Antiga

ISBN 978-88-6749-645-7

€ 22 / $ 25

The publisher would like to thank all
those who have kindly given their
permission for the reproduction of material for this book. Every effort has
been made to obtain permission to re-
produce the images and texts in this
catalogue. However, as is standard editorial policy, the publisher is at the
disposal of copyright holders and under-
takes to correct any omissions or
errors in future editions.

Co-produced with ONASSIS
CULTURE.

With kind support of UNA gallery,
Piacenza – Italy, Collezione La Gaia,
Busca – Italy, Valter Cassandro,
Michele Cristella, Callirrhoë, Athens,
OCEANIC PRO, ArtVolt, and My
Ionian Group.

**SALZBURGER
KUNSTVEREIN**

**ONASSIS
CULTURE**